Being with Jesus

Henry,

Congratulations on your graduation!! It is such a very important accomplishment and I am so proud of you. I am especially proud of how you continued to follow the Lord throughout High School. I am praying for you as you head to VT (I am super pumped) that you will find a community of guys that encourages you in your walk with the Lord. I also hope you find a good ministry where you can grow as well as use your gifts for His Kingdom. I pray that the Lord uses this book to keep you in God's word. Also, I want you to know that I am always here for you if you ever need me and I can't wait to hang out with you when you get here.

Jim Branch

By God's Grace,
Andrew

For Tim, Michelle, and Hunter. You are each such a gift and a treasure. We adore you, are so proud of you, and are so grateful God has given us the incredible privilege of being your parents. We love you! May you always know His great affection.

Contents

Preface   5

Introduction   7

1 – Beginning (John 1:1-18)   9

2 – What are you seeking? (John 1:35-42)   13

3 – The wedding (John 2:1-11)   17

4 – Jesus in solitude (Mark 1:32-39)   23

5 – Who do you say that I am? (Matthew 16:13-20)   28

6 – What is your name? (Mark 5:1-20)   34

7 – Daughter (Mark 5:24-34)   39

8 – The truth will set you free (John 8:31-32)   44

9 – The groan (Mark 7:31-37)   49

10 – The deeper issue (Mark 2:1-12)   53

11 – Do you want to get well? (John 5:1-9)   60

12 – Neither do I condemn you (John 8:2-11)   66

13 – To be celebrated (Luke 15:11-32)   72

14 – Like treasure (Matthew 13:44)   78

15 – Little lamb, arise! (Mark 5:21-24, 35-43)   82

16 – Born of the Spirit (John 2:23-3:8)   87

17 – Let down your nets for a catch (Luke 5:1-11)   92

18 – When you pray (Matthew 6:5-15)   97

19 – Abiding (John 15:1-8)   102

20 – Ordering our affections (Luke 10:38-42)   107

21 – Do you see anything? (Mark 8:22-26)   113

22 – She has done a beautiful thing (Mark 14:3-9)   118

23 – You give them something to eat (Mark 6:30-44)   123

24 – Rest (Matthew 11:28-30)   128

25 – Weeping and kissing (Luke 7:36-50)   132

26 – It is finished (John 19:28-30)   138

27 – Risen wounds (John 20:19-20)   142

28 – Do you truly love? (John 21:15-19)   147

29 – As the Father sent me (John 20:21-23)   152

30 – Strong toward (Acts 2:37-47)   156
Conclusion   161

Preface

This book is designed to be a thirty-day journey. A journey meant to take us more deeply into the life and ministry of Jesus. But it is also meant to be much more than that. My deepest hope is that, over the next thirty days, we will be taken more deeply into the very heart of Jesus. In order for that to happen we will need to pay very careful attention, both to him and to what he is doing within and among us. We will need to take our time and go slowly. We will need to linger when it is time to linger, and to sit and reflect when it is time to sit and reflect. Getting to know someone's heart takes time and space. We will need to listen carefully to his voice, to its tone and its inflection, in order to really hear what he is saying. We will need to look deeply into his eyes and see what they hold, both for the ones that are standing before him at any given moment, as well as for us. And we will do all of this in order that we might really see what is there to be seen and really hear what is there to be heard.

Therefore, it is my suggestion to take only one of these reflections per day and let it work on us, and in us, in every way possible. Chew on it thoroughly, savor every bit of its taste. Or, as the apostle Paul said so beautifully, "Let the word of Christ dwell in you richly." (Colossians 3:16) And at the end of our time together, who knows, maybe being with Jesus will have had a deep effect on our hearts and souls.

So wherever you are as we begin this journey — on a sabbatical or an extended vacation, at a camp or on a mission trip of some sort, or just at home going through your day-to-day routine — my hope is that it will meet you right where you are and offer you rich time and space to simply *be with Jesus* in a way that deeply transforms you. May you know his peace.

Jim

Introduction

There is a definite art to being with someone. It involves being fully present to them—open and attentive. It consists of listening to them and offering them space and room *to be*. It requires that we not be too occupied, or preoccupied, with other people or things and ultimately asks us to let go of our agendas and control. *Being with* someone involves a significant investment of time and focused stillness. It involves a deep shift of heart and mind; away from our constant obsession with *doing* to the freedom and joy of *being*.

That's what Jesus really wants—for us to simply be *with him*. In fact, that's where the entire spiritual life begins. When we learn the joy and delight of being with Jesus, then, and only then, will we have anything of value to offer our world. That is what true ministry is all about. In its purest form, ministry can only be an outward expression of a deep inner reality. Apart from that, apart from what God is doing within us, it is just smoke and mirrors. Apart from the life of his Spirit within us, we have absolutely nothing of substance to offer those in our world who are dying for anything of substance. *Being with Jesus* is the most important discipline in all of the spiritual life.

Nowhere is this more evident than in the calling of the disciples. (Mark 3) Jesus went up to the mountain and called to himself *those whom he desired*. The whole reason for this calling was so that *they might be with him and he might send them out to preach.* (Mark 3:14) Did you get that? Did you see the order? He called them *first* because he desired them *to be with him*, and then, as a result, so that he could send them out to preach. Jesus knew that there was something about the *being with* that would give power and authenticity to the *sending out*.

I don't know about you, but I'm pretty good at the *doing* part. It just seems to come naturally. I am not, however, very good at the *being* part. Therefore, I need plenty of practice; especially if the *being* part is where the *doing* part gets its strength. So, over the next thirty days, let's concentrate together on *being with Jesus*. And maybe, through *being with him*, we might find that our lives become more like his in the process.

1 – Beginning

Silence

Spend a few minutes in silence allowing your soul and spirit to come to stillness before God. This will prepare your heart to receive whatever he may have for you today.

Read

At the beginning God expressed himself. That personal expression, that word, was with God, and was God, and he existed with God from the beginning. All creation took place through him, and none took place without him. In him appeared life and this life was the light of mankind. The light still shines in the darkness and the darkness has never put it out.

A man called John was sent by God as a witness to the light, so that any man who heard his testimony might believe in the light. This man was not himself the light: he was sent simply as a personal witness to that light.

That was the true light which shines upon every man as he comes into the world. He came into the world – the world he had created – and the world failed to recognise him. He came into his own creation, and his own people would not accept him. Yet wherever men did accept him he gave them the power to become sons of God. These were the men who truly believed in him, and their birth depended not on the course of nature nor on any impulse or plan of man, but on God.

So the word of God became a human being and lived among us. We saw his splendour (the splendour as of a father's only son), full of grace and truth. And it was about him that John stood up and testified, exclaiming: "Here is the one I was speaking about when I said that although he would come after me he would always be in front of me; for he existed before I was born!" Indeed, every one of us has shared in his riches – there is a grace in our lives because of his grace. For while the Law was given by Moses, love and truth came through Jesus Christ. It is true that no one has ever seen God at any time. Yet the divine and only Son, who lives in the closest intimacy with the Father, has made him known. (John 1:1-18 JBP)

Questions for Reflection

What about this passage speaks deeply to something in your life or heart right now?

In what ways are you at a beginning point right now? How do you feel about that?

What are your deepest hopes, dreams, and expectations for this current season in your life?

Who has been the "word of God become human being" in your life these days? How?

How do you most deeply long for Jesus to "show up" in your life and world over the next thirty days?

Thoughts

Intimacy is the thing we all most deeply long for. And, if we are completely honest, it also scares us to death. Because intimacy, at its core, is about standing completely open and vulnerable — naked, if you will — before those whom we most deeply care about. This total openness brings with it the possibility that we may be loved and accepted in a way that we never dared to ask for or dream about. But, at the same time, it opens up the possibility that, when we are seen as we really are, we may also be rejected or hurt by those we most desperately long to be loved by. It is a risky proposition.

That's why there is something incredibly attractive and compelling about the picture John paints of Jesus. John tells us that before the foundations of the universe, before there was even a before, before all things, before time, Jesus was there. Not only was he there, but he was there *with* God in some mysterious and wonderfully intimate way. And not only was he there *with* God, but he, indeed, *was* God. Now that's intimacy! John says it so well when he says: "Yet the divine and only Son, who lives in the closest intimacy with the Father, has made him known."

That gives us hope. Hope that the intimacy we most deeply long for might actually be possible. Hope that this invitation to *be with Jesus* might be bigger than we can imagine. Hope that God is so full of love and intimacy that he created us out of the overflow of that passionate affection; that we might join in his great round dance of love. In fact, that's why we were made.

Pray
Simply try to *be with* Jesus for five minutes, no words, no requests, just sit in his presence and be with him and realize that he is with you. At the end of your time ask him how he wants you to "make him flesh" in your life and world today.

Respond
What is your response to your time *with Jesus* today? What is he doing in you right now? What is he asking of you? Spend a few minutes writing it down in the space that follows. And spend the last few minutes thanking him that he is the "word made flesh."

2 – What are you seeking?

Silence

Spend a few minutes in silence allowing your soul and spirit to come to stillness before God. This will prepare your heart to receive whatever he may have for you today.

Read

The next day again John was standing with two of his disciples, and he looked at Jesus as he walked by and said, "Behold, the Lamb of God!" The two disciples heard him say this, and they followed Jesus. Jesus turned and saw them following and said to them, "What are you seeking?" And they said to him, "Rabbi" (which means Teacher), "where are you staying?" He said to them, "Come and you will see." So they came and saw where he was staying, and they stayed with him that day, for it was about the tenth hour. One of the two who heard John speak and followed Jesus was Andrew, Simon Peter's brother. He first found his own brother Simon and said to him, "We have found the Messiah" (which means Christ). He brought him to Jesus. Jesus looked at him and said, "You are Simon the son of John. You shall be called Cephas" (which means Peter). (John 1:35-42 ESV)

Questions for Reflection

What about this story stands out to you? Why?

How does it intersect with your life right now?

What are you seeking?

What would it look like for you to *stay with him* today?

Who *brought you to Jesus*?

Whom might he want you to bring to him today? What does that look like?

Thoughts

Where are you staying? It seems a rather strange response to the question Jesus had just asked them, doesn't it? But maybe it is not so strange at all. The word for *stay* in the Greek is *meno*. In this passage it is translated "stay," but elsewhere in the New Testament it is translated remain, or abide. So it is a very telling word when used in this context. It is almost as if the disciples were saying, *"We really just want to be with you. That is the deepest longing of our hearts. Your very presence has touched something deep within us that we didn't even know was there and, more than anything, we just want to be with you if that's okay. Where are you staying?"*

And you have to love the answer Jesus gave: "Come and you will see." He was delighted! He was delighted because there was nothing he wanted more. For as much as we long to be with Jesus, he longs to be with us even more. Why else would he leave the Father's side, and the throne room of heaven, to come down to earth in the form of a man? So that he could be with us, and so that he could make a way (via the cross) for us to be *with* God. Isn't that incredible?

Do you find it hard to imagine that God truly desires you? Could it be possible that the God of the universe wants to be with you? Is it beyond your wildest dreams to think that your presence brings a smile to his face and joy to his heart? Well it does! You see, not only do we deeply desire to be with Jesus, but he deeply desires to be with us. Kind of changes things, doesn't it? Kind of lets us know that this is not a one-sided affair. When we come to the realization that Jesus not only loves us, but also desires to be with us, it does something wonderful deep within us. Something that kindles the fire of new affection in our hearts. Something that gives us new life and energy in the

deepest places of our soul. Something that makes us want
to spend every minute of every day in his presence.

Pray

What are the things weighing on your heart today that
Jesus longs for you to let him know about? Not so much
because he doesn't know them already (because he does),
but because the sharing of those things is what genuinely
being with someone is all about. Unburden yourself. Give
all that is on your heart to him and release it into his strong
and loving hands.

Respond

What is your response to your time *with Jesus* today? What
is he doing in your heart right now? What is he asking of
you? How will *being with* him impact the way you live
your life today? Spend a few minutes writing it down in
the space that follows.

3 – The wedding

Silence

Spend a few minutes in silence allowing your soul and spirit to come to stillness before God. This will prepare your heart to receive whatever he may have for you today.

Read

On the third day a wedding took place at Cana in Galilee. Jesus' mother was there, and Jesus and his disciples had also been invited to the wedding. When the wine was gone, Jesus' mother said to him, "They have no more wine."

"Woman, why do you involve me?" Jesus replied. "My hour has not yet come."

His mother said to the servants, "Do whatever he tells you."

Nearby stood six stone water jars, the kind used by the Jews for ceremonial washing, each holding from twenty to thirty gallons.

Jesus said to the servants, "Fill the jars with water"; so they filled them to the brim.

Then he told them, "Now draw some out and take it to the master of the banquet."

They did so, and the master of the banquet tasted the water that had been turned into wine. He did not realize where it had come from, though the servants who had drawn the water knew. Then he called the bridegroom aside and said, "Everyone brings out the choice wine first and then the cheaper wine after the guests have had too much to drink; but you have saved the best till now."

What Jesus did here in Cana of Galilee was the first of the signs through which he revealed his glory; and his disciples believed in him. (John 2:1-11 NIV)

Questions for Reflection

What in this passage catches your attention?

How does it speak to something in your heart or life?

Do you see Jesus as a person who was *invited* to special events? Why or why not?

Do you think there was something about him that was the reason he was invited to this wedding?

What do you think is significant about Jesus performing his first miracle at a wedding?

Why do you think he performed this miracle the way he did?

How would you have done it?

Why use the water jars?

How might Jesus want to transform your life the same way he did the wine?

Thoughts

I often wonder when I read this story how many people really knew what had just happened and how many people went right on with the party, completely oblivious to the fact that something miraculous had just taken place. Did anyone know, other than the servants that filled the stone jars with water and then took them to the master of the banquet? Mary obviously knew. And it seems probable that the disciples knew because John wrote that the miracle caused them to *believe in him*. But did they know because they saw it firsthand, or were they told about it afterwards?

And what a way to *reveal your glory*. If it were me, I would have made sure everyone knew what I had just done — you know, public announcement, news crews on the scene, dropping leaflets from the sky, that sort of thing. But not Jesus. He wanted to keep it quiet. He didn't seem to want anyone to know, probably not even the bride and groom.

There are many possible motives for this desire for secrecy, the most obvious of which is kindness. Jesus was trying to spare the families the embarrassment and humiliation of a major social faux pas. Another possible explanation for his reluctance to be more public at this time, some would say, had something to do with what has been called the Messianic Secret. Under this theory, Jesus chose secrecy so that his "time" (the things that would set the wheels in motion, ultimately leading to his suffering and death) wouldn't come faster than it was intended to. And while there is probably a good bit of truth to that theory as well, I think it might have been about something even bigger than that. I think it might have been about something that was lodged deeply within his soul and Spirit; the same thing that led him to empty himself and *make himself nothing, taking the very nature of a servant.* (Philippians 2:7) Or, as the King James Version says, to make himself *of no reputation.*

There seems to be something deep within the heart of God that loves the hidden, the small, the empty, the nothing, *the invisible.* In fact, there seems to be something deep within him that is actually drawn to it. And, just maybe, that is one of the major things that made the few people who actually saw what happened *believe in him.* Wouldn't you?

I mean what could be more beautiful than hearing Jesus tell the servants what he wanted them to do, seeing the amused look on his face as he watched them take the "wine" to the master of the banquet to be tasted, and then seeing the master of the banquet call the bridegroom aside and rave about the incredible quality of this newly created "best" wine. Just imagine the bridegroom standing there, scratching his head, wondering what in the world this man was talking about.

I would love to have been standing beside Jesus at that point. What do you think he did? I can imagine a smile, a wink, and a shrug of the shoulders as he says, "Well, back to the party" and turns casually to rejoin the festivities. A Jesus like that would truly capture my heart. What about yours? If nothing else it goes to show that we really have to keep our eyes on Jesus—he's sneaky. He is likely to do some of his very best work while no one is really paying attention. I love that about him. Don't you?

Pray
Pray that Jesus would give you eyes to see what he is up to in even the most unlikely ways, places, and people. Pray that he would grow in you a desire to serve him in small, hidden, invisible ways.

Respond

Write in the space that follows about some of the hidden things you have seen Jesus doing lately — and give him thanks. Now ask Jesus how he might want you to serve in a hidden way in the next 24 hours? Write that down as well. How are you doing three days into our adventure?

4 – Jesus in solitude

Silence

Spend a few minutes in silence allowing your soul and spirit to come to stillness before God. It is very important not to skip this part, it will prepare your heart to receive whatever he may have for you today.

Read

That evening after sunset the people brought to Jesus all the sick and demon-possessed. The whole town gathered at the door, and Jesus healed many who had various diseases. He also drove out many demons, but he would not let the demons speak because they knew who he was.

Very early in the morning, while it was still dark, Jesus got up, left the house and went off to a solitary place, where he prayed. Simon and his companions went to look for him, and when they found him, they exclaimed: "Everyone is looking for you!"

Jesus replied, "Let us go somewhere else – to the nearby villages – so I can preach there also. That is why I have come." So he traveled throughout Galilee, preaching in their synagogues and driving out demons. (Mark 1:32-39 NIV)

Questions for Reflection

Who, or what, determines how you live your life each day?

Who, or what, determined that for Jesus?

When you get super busy, what does it do to you? What does it do within you?

When many demands are being made of you, how do you choose which ones get top priority?

What, or who, helps you determine which things are important and which are merely urgent?

What does your daily rhythm of being with Jesus look like?

Thoughts

A wise saint once said, "Only he who obeys a rhythm superior to his own is free." Nowhere do we see that particular principle more clearly modeled out than here in the gospel of Mark.

Jesus was in Capernaum with his disciples teaching in the synagogue, driving out demons, and healing the sick and broken. Word was spreading quickly. His popularity was exploding. Everyone wanted to get a peek at this miracle worker who seemed to have power and authority that hadn't been seen for centuries. As a matter of fact, as evening arrived the entire town was lined up at his door— each in search of his or her own miracle. And, we are told, *Jesus healed many*. Literally, what Mark tells us is that Jesus healed a *great number*. It must've taken forever, surely lasting into the wee hours of the morning. And as the last person was healed and the doors were closed, Jesus and his disciples had to have been completely exhausted.

Yet, the very next morning, *while it was still dark*, Jesus got up, left the house, and went to a solitary place to be *with* his Father. It was just what he did. It was wired into the very fabric of his being. Does that mean it was easy?

Absolutely not! But it does mean that it was incredibly important because Jesus (yes, even Jesus) operated by a rhythm superior to his own. He realized that if he was to accomplish the mission he was sent to earth to accomplish, he *must* make time and space to be with his Father: to listen to him, to speak with him, to be filled by him, to be guided and directed by him. It was a must.

So he got up and went off into solitude. He drew near to God. And, as a result of this practice, he received direction and guidance for the day ahead. In fact, when the disciples find him and tell him that everyone is looking for him, he responds by saying that he must now go *somewhere else — to the nearby villages — so he can preach there also.* That's why he came in the first place. You see, the time that Jesus had just spent with his Father had guided and directed his steps for the day ahead. It determined his rhythm in spite of all of the needs and demands that were pressing in on him. He didn't allow the content of his days to be determined by urgent demands, but only by the voice and presence of his Father.

May it always be the same with us. May we always obey a rhythm superior to our own — the rhythm of Jesus. May our steps always be ordered and determined by his love and his kingdom rather than our own agendas and compulsions. And may there be a deep shift within us; a shift from leading to being led. Because *only he who obeys a rhythm superior to his own is free.*

Pray

Ask God what his desires are for your day. What would he like for you to do? Who does he desire you to spend time with? Ask him to let your day and your agenda flow out of your time with him.

Respond

Spend some time reflecting on the idea of who or what regulates the way you spend your days. Write a little about what you think operating by God's rhythm and agenda might look like.

5 – Who do you say that I am?

Silence

Spend a few minutes in silence allowing your soul and spirit to come to stillness before God. Stillness allows your heart to be attentive and responsive to whatever God might have to say to you today.

Read

When Jesus arrived in the villages of Caesarea Philippi, he asked his disciples, "What are people saying about who the Son of Man is?"

They replied, "Some think he is John the Baptizer, some say Elijah, some Jeremiah or one of the other prophets."

He pressed them, "And how about you? Who do you say I am?"

Simon Peter said, "You're the Christ, the Messiah, the Son of the living God."

Jesus came back, "God bless you, Simon, son of Jonah! You didn't get that answer out of books or from teachers. My Father in heaven, God himself, let you in on this secret of who I really am. And now I'm going to tell you who you are, really are. You are Peter, a rock. This is the rock on which I will put together my church, a church so expansive with energy that not even the gates of hell will be able to keep it out.

"And that's not all. You will have complete and free access to God's kingdom, keys to open any and every door: no more barriers between heaven and earth, earth and heaven. A yes on earth is yes in heaven. A no on earth is no in heaven."

He swore the disciples to secrecy. He made them promise they would tell no one that he was the Messiah. (Matthew 16:13-20, The Message)

Questions for Reflection

Who do you say Jesus is? Not the church answers, or someone else's answer that you think sounds good, but *your* answer.

What makes you say that?

What is your picture of God? Of Jesus? How are they different? How are they similar?

Where does your picture of God come from? How accurate is it?

How does your picture of God, and of Jesus, affect the way you live?

Thoughts

A. W. Tozer once said that *what comes into our minds when we think about God may be the most important thing about us.* I think that's because he knew what a significant role our images of God play in the way we live our lives. For instance, if our image of him is that of a distant, disinterested, irrelevant figure, then what conceivable reason would we have to even want to have a relationship with him to begin with (or he with us for that matter)? In that scenario we better take matters into our own hands because everything is up to us and we can count on absolutely no help from him.

Or, if our image of God is that of a stern, angry and demanding figure, that creates another set of questions and issues. In that case our lives are likely to be filled with a fearful performing; always trying to earn his favor while attempting to keep away from condemnation.

There are a multitude of images we might have of God, each with its own set of behaviors that correlate directly with the images that we hold in our minds and hearts. Jesus obviously knew this as well, why else would he ask Simon Peter this question? After all, being the *visible image of the invisible God* (Colossians 1:15), one of his chief reasons for coming to earth in the first place was to confront all of our false images of God, deconstruct them, and replace them with truthful ones. That's why the writer of Hebrews reminds us that Jesus is *the radiance of God's glory and the exact representation of his being.* (Hebrews 1:3) All of our images of God should then be embodied in the life and character and heart of Jesus. So, when he asks Peter this question, he does not do so flippantly, but with great purpose and intention. He is trying to get to the root of the issue. Who do we really say that he is?

It is almost as if the question itself holds up a mirror to our lives, so that we can actually see what our lives tell us about who we really believe Jesus to be. For instance, if our lives are full of worry and anxiety, what does that tell us about what we really believe to be true about him? Or, if our lives are full of fear and insecurity, what does that say about what we truly believe? Or if our lives are consumed with busyness, hurry, and rush, what does that tell us about our image of him? For, at its heart, this is really a diagnostic question.

That is what is so beautiful about Peter's answer — it comes right from the core of his being. "You're the Christ, the Messiah, the Son of the living God," he replies, not fully knowing the depths of the answer he is uttering. *You are the One we have been waiting for and watching for and hoping for. You are the One, sent from God to deliver us from sin and oppression and bondage. You are God in the flesh!* And Jesus recognizes that even though Peter doesn't fully understand what he's saying — and will not for some time — he has gotten a little glimpse of the truth. Truth that he didn't come up with on his own, but truth that was wonderfully and mysteriously revealed to him by God. Simon Peter would spend the rest of his life trying to figure out all that his answer meant, but he was definitely heading in the right direction.

And so, now it is our turn to answer. Who do we say Jesus is? Are we truly able to utter Simon Peter's response; which is fine if it is authentic within us? Or do we need to do some soul-searching, some reflecting, and some praying in hopes that God might give us a similar revelation? That he might give us an answer that we too can spend our entire lives coming to understand.

Pray

Ask God to show you who he is today. Ask him for a window — an experience, a person, a scripture, or a metaphor — that will give you a beautiful picture of who he really is. Also, pray that he will give you eyes to see that the way you live your life tells you a lot about what you really believe to be true about him. Ask him to deconstruct all of the images within you that simply aren't true, and to replace them with ones that are.

Respond

Draw your current picture of God in the space below.

6 – What is your name?

Silence

Spend a few minutes in silence allowing your heart and soul to be still before God. Stillness allows you to be awake and attentive to God and to whatever he might want to say to you today.

Read

They went across the lake to the region of the Gerasenes. When Jesus got out of the boat, a man with an impure spirit came from the tombs to meet him. This man lived in the tombs, and no one could bind him anymore, not even with a chain. For he had often been chained hand and foot, but he tore the chains apart and broke the irons on his feet. No one was strong enough to subdue him. Night and day among the tombs and in the hills he would cry out and cut himself with stones.

When he saw Jesus from a distance, he ran and fell on his knees in front of him. He shouted at the top of his voice, "What do you want with me, Jesus, Son of the Most High God? In God's name don't torture me!" For Jesus had said to him, "Come out of this man, you impure spirit!"

Then Jesus asked him, "What is your name?"

"My name is Legion," he replied, "for we are many." And he begged Jesus again and again not to send them out of the area.

A large herd of pigs was feeding on the nearby hillside. The demons begged Jesus, "Send us among the pigs; allow us to go into them." He gave them permission, and the impure spirits came out and went into the pigs. The herd, about two thousand in number, rushed down the steep bank into the lake and were drowned.

Those tending the pigs ran off and reported this in the town and countryside, and the people went out to see what had happened. When they came to Jesus, they saw the man who had been possessed by the legion of demons, sitting there, dressed and in his right mind; and they were afraid. Those who had seen it told the people what had happened to the demon-possessed man – and told about the pigs as well. Then the people began to plead with Jesus to leave their region.

As Jesus was getting into the boat, the man who had been demon-possessed begged to go with him. Jesus did not let him, but said, "Go home to your own people and tell them how much the Lord has done for you, and how he has had mercy on you." So the man went away and began to tell in the Decapolis how much Jesus had done for him. And all the people were amazed. (Mark 5:1-20 NIV)

Questions for Reflection

What in this story speaks to something in your heart or life right now? How?

What do you notice about the man?

How can you relate to him?

What do you notice about Jesus?

Why do you think he asks the man his name?

What is the significance of the man's answer?

Pay attention to the transformation that occurs in him. What words describe him before? After?

If you had to pick a new name for the man after the transformation, what would it be?

Thoughts

What is your name? Another great question by Jesus. A question that, on the surface, seems fairly harmless and safe, but is actually one of incredible depth and insight. Because a person's name can tell us a lot about them, which was especially true in Jesus' day. A name was significant because it was meant to convey not just what a person was called, but who they really were. It was meant to tell us something about their identity; to give us a hint as to who they really believed themselves to be.

So when Jesus asks the name of this tortured soul, he is really asking, "Who are you? Who do you believe yourself to be?" And that is a great question. An important question. A question we all, at some point in our lives, must struggle to find an answer to. Who am I, really? How do I define myself? What is it that gives me a true sense of identity? What am I counting on to give me the worth and the value I deeply long for?

Most of us work our entire lives to find an answer to that question — to try and make a name for ourselves. The problem is that any name we *make* for ourselves can never be our true name. Because our true identity can never be achieved, it can only be bestowed. And it can only be bestowed by the One who made us.

"*My name is Legion,*" says this tortured soul, "*for we are many.*" In other words, "*I have no idea who I am. There are so many different voices in here that it's impossible to tell.*" A legion was around 5,000 soldiers, so obviously bearing that name meant that this man was a mass of chaos and confusion within. He was everybody. And because he was everybody, he was really nobody at all. That is undoubtedly the way he must have felt: insignificant, worthless, unlovable, a nobody. He was destined for a life of confusion, despair, and loneliness *because we all tend to live out of the name we most believe to be true about us.*

This is the man who comes down out of the tombs to meet Jesus on this particular day: a man who spends his life among the dead, cutting himself with stones, breaking chains, and crying out for some sort of relief from his torment. And while everyone else is running away from him, Jesus meets him right where he is, right in the middle of his pain and brokenness. And somehow, in the process, Legion is Legion no more—he receives a brand new name and, therefore, a brand new identity and a brand new life. He is completely and totally transformed.

Pray

Ask God to show you this day the name that you tend to live out of that is just not true. Maybe it is a name someone, at some point in your life, has actually called you that has caused you a great deal of pain. Or maybe it is a name that you came up with on your own as a result of the circumstances of your life.

Respond

Write your false name down in the space below and realize it for the lie that it is. That is not who you are! God has a new name that he longs to give you, one he wants you to live by from here on.

7 – Daughter

Silence

Spend a few minutes in silence allowing your heart and soul to be still before God. Rest in his presence. Allow the stillness to awaken you to his voice and his Spirit.

Read

A large crowd followed and pressed around him. And a woman was there who had been subject to bleeding for twelve years. She had suffered a great deal under the care of many doctors and had spent all she had, yet instead of getting better she grew worse. When she heard about Jesus, she came up behind him in the crowd and touched his cloak, because she thought, "If I just touch his clothes, I will be healed." Immediately her bleeding stopped and she felt in her body that she was freed from her suffering.

At once Jesus realized that power had gone out from him. He turned around in the crowd and asked, "Who touched my clothes?"

"You see the people crowding against you," his disciples answered, "and yet you can ask, 'Who touched me?' "

But Jesus kept looking around to see who had done it. Then the woman, knowing what had happened to her, came and fell at his feet and, trembling with fear, told him the whole truth. He said to her, "Daughter, your faith has healed you. Go in peace and be freed from your suffering." (Mark 5:24-34 NIV)

Questions for Reflection

What do you think it would be like to have something broken inside you for twelve years?

What effect do think it would have on your heart and soul?

Is there an area of brokenness in your life that has been a source of pain for a long time? What is it? What effect has it had on you?

What about this story captures your heart? Why?

What is significant about *how* Jesus healed this woman?

What is significant about what he said to her?

How are his words to her also his words to you today?

Thoughts

For twelve long years she had been broken inside. For twelve long years a continual bleeding had been her constant companion. For twelve long years she had been alone and isolated, the result of having such an affliction. Even her family could not be around her. For twelve long years she had seen the stares and the pointing. She had heard the whispers, the names she was called: outcast, freak, loser, and, the worst one of all, unclean. In fact, she had heard the names for so long that she had actually begun to believe that they were true. They had just become a part of life, a painful reality. They had become her identity.

She had tried everything to fix her problem, but it had only gotten worse. Now she was at the end of her rope, so she worked up the courage and pushed her way through the crowd, coming up behind Jesus. Maybe he could do for her what he had already done for so many others. She reached out and touched the edge of his robe. And instantly she knew that something miraculous had happened deep within her. She had been healed.

Jesus stopped in the middle of the crowded street, knowing something significant had just happened. Their eyes met as she came forward — delight in his, tears of relief in hers. She fell at his feet and told him the whole story. And after he listened intently to all that she had to say, he knelt down and lifted her chin with his hands. He looked deeply into her eyes and said, *"Daughter, your faith has healed you. Go in peace and be freed from your suffering."*

Almost as if to say, "You are not broken. You are not an outcast. You are not a loser. You are not unclean. That is no longer who you are. You are *mine*! You are *my daughter*. You are *my delight*. From now on that is your identity. From now on that is your name. A name that will give you the healing and the peace and the freedom you most deeply long for. From now on live your life out of that name."

And it is the same for you and for me. No longer are we to live out of those names that have brought us so much pain and hurt and grief through the years. That is not who we are. We are *His*! You and I are his daughters and his sons. We are the beloved of the Father. From now on that is the truth that is meant to give us the value and the worth we so desperately long for.

Pray
Today, in prayer, listen to the voice of the One who calls you his beloved.

Respond
Write down the word "Mine" below. That is what God calls you. Live this day in the knowledge and awareness that you are deeply, passionately, and extravagantly loved by your God.

8 – The truth will set you free

Silence

Spend a few minutes in silence allowing your heart and soul to be still before God. This will allow you to be aware of his presence and attentive to his voice—the voice of truth that can set you free.

Read

Jesus said to the people who believed in him, "You are truly my disciples if you remain faithful to my teachings. And you will know the truth, and the truth will set you free." (John 8:31-32 NLT)

Questions for Reflection

What word would you use to describe your life these days? Why?

How would you define the word freedom?

Where in your life are you experiencing freedom?

Where are you not experiencing freedom? Why?

How does freedom come about?

What is the relationship between truth and freedom?

Thoughts

Years ago, I was sitting with two high school friends at a local restaurant talking about life and faith and how we can live more authentically and intimately with Jesus. We were looking at these verses in John 8, about truth and freedom, when one of the guys had a bit of an epiphany. He looked up from his bible, turned to us, and said, "So what you are telling me is that if I am not free it is because I'm believing something that's not true?" And we all stopped for a minute, reflecting on what he had just said.

"That's exactly what I'm saying," I responded. "As a matter of fact I couldn't have said it any better myself." Somehow in his own beautifully simple way, he had taken a profound theological truth and made it incredibly practical. So much so that I still remember it to this day. In fact, whenever I am feeling particularly tied up or bound by something that I can't quite put my finger on I will ask myself, "Since I am not feeling free at this moment, what am I believing that is not true?" Because the truth always sets us free.

Freedom can be an elusive thing. Or maybe it's not elusive at all. Maybe it is the *believing* part that makes it seem elusive. Because we all have a tendency to believe things regularly that simply aren't true. The funny thing is that oftentimes they seem true, as we have seen since our journey began with our images of God, as well as our images of ourselves.

When we are able to get down to the truth, to deconstruct those narratives (the stories we live by) that are not true and replace them with the narratives of Jesus (the way, the truth, and the life), then we will finally be able to experience a sense of freedom in our lives. That's exactly what happened for *Legion*. That is also what happened for the bleeding woman. They both came face to face with the truth—Jesus. And when they came face to face with the truth, they were both set free.

What about us? What are we believing these days that is simply not true. What narratives are we living by that need to be deconstructed? And, as we spend time *with Jesus*, how does his truth begin to heal us and give us the freedom and the wholeness we most deeply long for?

Pray

Ask God to help you see the narratives you are living by that simply aren't true. And ask him to deconstruct those narratives and replace them with the truth—the narratives of Jesus.

Respond

In the space that follows, write down any narratives you are living by that are simply not true.

Now write down the truth; what Jesus has to say about that part of your life.

9 – The groan

Silence

Spend some time in silence allowing your heart and soul to come to rest. Just be fully present to God and to whatever he might want to do or say.

Read

Then he left the region of Tyre, went through Sidon back to Galilee Lake and over to the district of the Ten Towns. Some people brought a man who could neither hear nor speak and asked Jesus to lay a healing hand on him. He took the man off by himself, put his fingers in the man's ears and some spit on the man's tongue. Then Jesus looked up in prayer, groaned mightily, and commanded, "Ephphatha! – Open up!" And it happened. The man's hearing was clear and his speech plain – just like that.

Jesus urged them to keep it quiet, but they talked it up all the more, beside themselves with excitement. "He's done it all and done it well. He gives hearing to the deaf, speech to the speechless." (Mark 7:31-37, The Message)

Questions for Reflection

What do you think life was like for this man?

What do you think would have been the hardest part?

Why do you think Jesus *groaned mightily*?

What things in your life cause you to groan?

What things in your life cause Jesus to groan?

What do you think about a God who groans *with* us?

Thoughts

It is amazing how one little phrase can make so much difference, if we are paying careful attention. In this passage it is the phrase *groaned mightily.* Jesus is sitting with a man who can neither hear, nor speak. He has pulled him aside, taken him away from the crowds, realizing fully that this poor soul has felt like the center of attention long enough — and for all of the wrong reasons. Now he gently puts his healing hands on the very places that have caused this man so many years of pain — his ears and his tongue. Then he looks up to heaven and what does he do? He *groans.* What is that all about? And what are we to do with a God who groans?

The scriptures talk about groaning in several places. The apostle Paul tells us that all of creation *groans as in the pains of childbirth* (Romans 8:18-22), *waiting in eager expectation for the children of God to be revealed.* He then goes on to tell us that *we ourselves, who have the firstfruits of the Spirit, groan inwardly as we wait eagerly for our adoption to sonship.* (Romans 8:23) He expands on this particular groaning when he writes, "*Meanwhile we groan, longing to be clothed instead with our heavenly dwelling, because when we are clothed, we will not be found naked. For while we are in this tent, we groan and are burdened, because we do not wish to be unclothed but to be clothed instead with our heavenly dwelling, so that what is mortal may be swallowed up by life.*" (2 Corinthians 5:2-4) And finally Paul tells us that God himself even groans: *the Spirit himself intercedes for us with groans too deep for words.* (Romans 8:26) God groans for us. I think this is the kind of groaning that we see here in Mark 7.

Jesus sees a man whose life is filled with an enormous amount of pain and brokenness. And deep in his heart he is saddened by the thought that *this is not the way it was intended to be. It did not have to be like this.* His heart is broken over the pain and suffering of one of his dearly loved creations. So he groans. It is a groan filled with sadness and frustration. It is a groan that is also, at its core, filled with love and compassion.

What do you think about a God who groans? What do you think about a God who is heartbroken over our pain and brokenness? What do you think about a God who can't keep his hands off of us, but longs to touch us deeply in the very places that have caused us the most pain; bringing them back to wholeness and fullness (creation intent) once again?

Pray
Tell God about the things in your life that make you groan right now. Listen to him as he groans along with you. Now ask him to put his healing hands on those places of your life and begin a process of healing and wholeness.

Respond
Pay attention today for anyone who might be groaning somehow. Write their name(s) down in the space that follows, with a prayer for them to know God's comforting presence and healing touch in the midst of their groaning and pain.

10 – The deeper issue

Silence

Spend some time in silence allowing your heart and soul to come to rest. Just be fully present to God, aware of his presence, and attentive to his voice.

Read

A few days later, when Jesus again entered Capernaum, the people heard that he had come home. They gathered in such large numbers that there was no room left, not even outside the door, and he preached the word to them. Some men came, bringing to him a paralyzed man, carried by four of them. Since they could not get him to Jesus because of the crowd, they made an opening in the roof above Jesus by digging through it and then lowered the mat the man was lying on. When Jesus saw their faith, he said to the paralyzed man, "Son, your sins are forgiven."

Now some teachers of the law were sitting there, thinking to themselves, "Why does this fellow talk like that? He's blaspheming! Who can forgive sins but God alone?"

Immediately Jesus knew in his spirit that this was what they were thinking in their hearts, and he said to them, "Why are you thinking these things? Which is easier: to say to this paralyzed man, 'Your sins are forgiven,' or to say, 'Get up, take your mat and walk'? But I want you to know that the Son of Man has authority on earth to forgive sins." So he said to the man, "I tell you, get up, take your mat and go home." He got up, took his mat and walked out in full view of them all. This amazed everyone and they praised God, saying, "We have never seen anything like this!" (Mark 2:1-12 NIV)

Questions for Reflection

What do think it would've been like to have been this paralyzed man?

What do you think it would've been like to be his friends, the ones who carried his mat to Jesus?

What would your reaction have been to hearing the words, *your sins are forgiven*?

What are the patterns and habits in your life and/or heart that cause you to feel paralyzed spiritually?

How do these things show themselves in your life?

What is at the root of these patterns and habits?

Thoughts

Imagine the scene. Imagine being paralyzed for who knows how long. Imagine a bunch of your friends devising a plan to get you to the feet of Jesus. Imagine being one of the friends carrying the mat. What do you think it would've been like to be on this journey? What do you think the main motivation of the friends was? They must have cared deeply for this paralyzed man to have dreamt up such a scheme. We are not told how many of them there were, only that four of them were carrying him. Were there more than four? Did they switch off, or did these four carry him the whole way? And how far did they have to go? It must have been an exhausting journey.

And imagine getting to the house and realizing that you can't get inside. What then? Who was the one who came up with the idea of going up on the roof? And how do you think the homeowner felt about that when he saw pieces of his roof falling to the floor? And after all of the hurdles were cleared, and their friend finally laid at Jesus' feet, how did they feel when they heard what he said? "Son, your sins are forgiven." They must have been thinking, "It's his legs. The problem is with his legs."

But Jesus knew better. Jesus knew that the real problem was much deeper than just his legs. Because his paralysis was only a symptom of a much larger issue—as it is with each of us. Our paralysis, most likely, is not physical like this particular man's, but it is no less a reality. Our paralysis is most likely emotional and, ultimately, spiritual. But at the root of this paralysis, as with the man in Mark 2, lies the issue of sin. The two are intimately linked.

I do not know what your paralysis looks like, it is a little different for everyone it seems, but I am pretty aware of my own. I usually recognize it only after it has been going on for a while. Only after the gravitational pull of the old self towards darkness, depression, loneliness, and sadness has been going on for a few days or weeks and I am beginning to feel a little stuck. It is a downward spiral really, but a slow one that I do not recognize until a good bit of life and energy has already drained out of me. Maybe the most telling sign is a feeling that I have lost some sense of being able to "get up and walk." It's like something has grabbed hold of me and is weighing me down, and "getting up" — whatever that may look like — feels like an impossible task. And it is a feeling that only seems to gain momentum; the longer it lasts, the stronger it seems to become.

Luckily Jesus knows the link between, "*Your sins are forgiven*" and "*Get up, take your mat and walk.*" He knows that the deeper issue must be taken care of before the more surface issues can be resolved. He says to me, "*Son, your sins are forgiven,*" just the way he did to the paralyzed man. He reminds me that, first and foremost, I am his son and he loves me immensely. This knowledge empowers me by speaking to the *true self* that he has created me to be. This truth cuts right to my core, reminding me of who I truly am, as well as who I am not. His love and his forgiveness then offer me the strength and ability to do what he desires for me the most: *get up, take up my mat and walk.* It is as if he were saying to me: "*Do not sit any longer in this helpless paralysis, for I have given you my love and my forgiveness, which breaks the chains of your powerlessness and allows you the ability to rise and leave the mat, and the paralysis, behind and walk in newness of life.*"

Therefore I must listen to his call daily to do just that. And I must respond. I must consistently choose, by his power, to *get up.* In the process, I also need to pay careful attention to the typical patterns of my heart and soul and constantly be asking myself several diagnostic questions: When am I at my best spiritually? When I am thriving spiritually, what factors are consistently present? When am I at my worst? And what factors contribute most significantly to that? What are my warning signs that I am slipping into darkness and spiritual paralysis? What are the things I must do regularly to create the space that helps keep me (by God's grace) in a good spiritual place?

And then, in the end, maybe my result will be much like this man's: *He got up, took his mat and walked out in full view of them all. This amazed everyone and they praised God, saying, "We have never seen anything like this!"* Thanks be to God!

Pray
Pray that God would make you aware today of the deeper issues of your heart and soul. Pray for his power and strength to enable you to "get up," whatever that may look like.

Respond
Write down the deeper issues of your heart and soul in the space below. Sometime today share these things with someone else. Ask them to pray with you and for you, to help you, as they are able, in the process of God raising you up.

11 – Do you want to get well?

Silence

Spend a few minutes in silence allowing your soul and spirit to come to stillness before God. This will prepare your heart both to hear and to receive whatever he may have for you today.

Read

Some time later, Jesus went up to Jerusalem for one of the Jewish festivals. Now there is in Jerusalem near the Sheep Gate a pool, which in Aramaic is called Bethesda and which is surrounded by five covered colonnades. Here a great number of disabled people used to lie – the blind, the lame, the paralyzed. One who was there had been an invalid for thirty-eight years. When Jesus saw him lying there and learned that he had been in this condition for a long time, he asked him, "Do you want to get well?"

"Sir," the invalid replied, "I have no one to help me into the pool when the water is stirred. While I am trying to get in, someone else goes down ahead of me."

Then Jesus said to him, "Get up! Pick up your mat and walk." At once the man was cured; he picked up his mat and walked.

The day on which this took place was a Sabbath, and so the Jewish leaders said to the man who had been healed, "It is the Sabbath; the law forbids you to carry your mat."

But he replied, "The man who made me well said to me, 'Pick up your mat and walk.'"

So they asked him, "Who is this fellow who told you to pick it up and walk?"

The man who was healed had no idea who it was, for Jesus had slipped away into the crowd that was there.

Later Jesus found him at the temple and said to him, "See, you are well again. Stop sinning or something worse may happen to you." The man went away and told the Jewish leaders that it was Jesus who had made him well. (John 5:1-15)

Questions for Reflection

Does *"Do you want to get well?"* seem like an odd question to you, given the context? Why, or why not?

Why might this man not want to get well?

What might change about his life if he did get well?

If Jesus were to ask you that question right now, what would your answer be?

What do you need to get well from?

Are you willing? Why or why not?

Is there something you need to leave behind?

Thoughts

Jesus and his disciples had arrived at Jerusalem for a feast; a time to remember and to celebrate all that God had done in the life of Israel. It was an exciting season, the city was abuzz, filled with people and life and energy. And, as they entered the city, one of the first places they went was a pool near the Sheep Gate called Bethesda — which meant House of Mercy.

Maybe they went there because Jesus, being *the Lamb of God who takes away the sin of the world*, couldn't stay away from the Sheep Gate. Or maybe they went there because the people that were gathered around the pool — the broken, the desperate, the outcast, the hurting — were the ones who had really captured his heart. My guess is that it was a place he just couldn't stay away from. Or maybe they went there for a more specific reason. Maybe it was because he knew that there was someone lying by the pool that he needed to see.

Whatever the reason, Jesus and his friends arrived at this pool; a place where masses of disabled people gathered each day in hopes of being made whole — one of whom, we are told, had been there 38 years. It was this man who caught Jesus' eye this day. I wonder what *it* was that made Jesus fix his eyes upon this particular man? Was it his story? Was it something in his look? Was it his voice? Or maybe his attitude? The one thing we do know is that Jesus had a very unique way of seeing. In fact, the word used here to describe how Jesus saw this man is *eido*, which means to see right to the very core of something; to perceive. Jesus didn't just *see* this man, he *saw into* this man. That's what captured him.

And that's what made him ask this seemingly ridiculous question: "Do you want to get well?" I mean, why in the world would someone who had been an invalid for 38 years not want to get well? It seems like an absurd question. But, if we are perfectly honest, we realize that it is not an absurd question at all. In fact, it is incredibly profound. It is profound because as full as our lives are of dysfunction and chaos and brokenness and pain, we are still, for some strange reason, afraid of and resistant to change.

We, like this man, have grown so used to "life on the mat" that any other kind of life scares us to death. Somehow we have become oddly comfortable in our disability and/or dysfunction. Somewhere along the way we have accepted that this pattern—this way of being—is *just the way life is,* so we have learned to accept it and live with it. We have settled. We have decided that things are never going to get any better, so we settle down and settle into our unhealthy habits and patterns and addictions. We settle for far less than what God truly desires for us.

But God calls us to much more than that. He calls us to much more than what we are willing to settle for. He calls us to fullness. He calls us to wholeness. He calls us to obedience. He calls us to leave behind whatever "story" we have been content to *live in,* that is less than what he wants for (and from) us, and to follow him fully and completely. He calls us to "Get up! Pick up our mat and walk!" What does that look like for you? What is the "story" God is calling you to leave behind? What is the "mat" he is calling you to get up from and come and follow him? Are you willing?

Pray
Ask God to show you today if there is some "story" or some "mat" that he wants you to leave behind. Ask him for the strength and the courage to do so.

Response

In the space below, spend some time writing your response to the question, "Do you want to get well?"

12 – Neither do I condemn you

Silence

Spend a few minutes in silence allowing your heart and soul to be still before God. Rest in his presence. Allow the stillness to awaken you to his voice and his Spirit.

Read

Early in the morning he came again to the temple. All the people came to him, and he sat down and taught them. The scribes and the Pharisees brought a woman who had been caught in adultery, and placing her in the midst they said to him, "Teacher, this woman has been caught in the act of adultery. Now in the Law Moses commanded us to stone such women. So what do you say?" This they said to test him, that they might have some charge to bring against him. Jesus bent down and wrote with his finger on the ground. And as they continued to ask him, he stood up and said to them, "Let him who is without sin among you be the first to throw a stone at her." And once more he bent down and wrote on the ground. But when they heard it, they went away one by one, beginning with the older ones, and Jesus was left alone with the woman standing before him. Jesus stood up and said to her, "Woman, where are they? Has no one condemned you?" She said, "No one, Lord." And Jesus said, "Neither do I condemn you; go, and from now on sin no more." (John 8:2-11 ESV)

Questions for Reflection

Where do you find yourself in this story? Why?

Who can you relate to the most? How?

How would you define the word *condemn*?

When and how have you felt condemned recently?

How do you tend to condemn yourself?

What do the words *neither do I condemn you* do in you?

Thoughts

Neither do I condemn you. As I read these words they almost leap off the page; or my heart almost leaps out of my chest, I'm not exactly sure which. Either way, they bring me to life inside. You see, I often tend to have condemnation issues. Not so much on the giving end as on the receiving end. And the funny thing is that I'm not sure I would've called it that until I read this word. And as soon as I saw it my heart and soul quickly said, "That's it! That's what I experience so often." It doesn't really take much — an unfavorable comparison, a criticism received, an insecurity struck — and the next thing you know I am at the bottom of a pit. You know, the pit of despair and depression that these things tend to send us right to the bottom of; or at least they do me.

The word condemn means *to express an unfavorable or adverse judgment on; to indicate strong disapproval; to pronounce guilty.* The Greek word *katakrino* means *to give judgment against.* It is a positional word; a word that is intended to lessen the condemned and heighten the condemner. It is a word that creates a dichotomy between the judger and the judged.

That definitely comes to life in John 8. The scribes and Pharisees bring the adulterous woman before Jesus, rocks firmly in hand, fully intending to stone her to death. They the high and holy and she the sinful and lowly. But, as he always seems to do, Jesus so beautifully turns the tables. He levels the playing field. "Let him who is without sin among you be the first to throw a stone at her," he says. And one by one, oldest first, they all leave with the harsh realization that "*we* are no better than she is. *We* are not above her."

So, in the end, there is Jesus, alone with this woman in the middle of what used to be a crowded street. He stands up from writing on the ground, looks tenderly into her eyes and says, "Where are they? Has no one condemned you?"

"No. No one, Lord," she replies, eyes downcast, wondering what the next words from his lips might be. Would they be words of rebuke? Words of condemnation or judgment? That is probably what she expects. But to her surprise — and delight — the words he gives her are words of life, not death. "Neither do I condemn you; go, and sin no more." *Neither do I condemn you.* I'll bet those words were music to her soul. I know they are to mine.

It is almost as if Jesus is saying: *Since I do not condemn you, do not allow others (including yourself) that power either. When you do that, you give people and things and events and circumstances a power over you that they neither have, nor deserve. Do not do that. Do not let the voices within (or without) convince you that you are any less than the Beloved of the Father. Do not allow comparison, or criticism, or insecurity to drag you down into the pit of condemnation. Instead, live your life out of the joy and gratitude and freedom of being loved. For God did not send his son into the world to condemn the world, but to save the world through him. (John 3:17) Or,* as The Message puts it: *God didn't go to all the trouble of sending his Son merely to point an accusing finger, telling the world how bad it was. He came to help, to put the world right again.* Thanks be to him!

Pray

Ask God to show you how you might be living in condemnation. Ask him to show you who you might be holding under condemnation. Listen to his words in John 8:11, they are for you. Thank him for his forgiveness and his love.

Respond

Write a little, in the space that follows, about what God has shown you today about condemnation, be it of yourself or of others.

How do you need to stop condemning yourself? How do you need to stop condemning others? Who, specifically, does that involve?

13 – To be celebrated

Silence

Spend a few minutes in silence allowing your heart and soul to come to rest. Sit in God's presence and enjoy his great affection for you. Ask him to be with you in this time.

Read

Jesus continued: "There was a man who had two sons. The younger one said to his father, 'Father, give me my share of the estate.' So he divided his property between them.

"Not long after that, the younger son got together all he had, set off for a distant country and there squandered his wealth in wild living. After he had spent everything, there was a severe famine in that whole country, and he began to be in need. So he went and hired himself out to a citizen of that country, who sent him to his fields to feed pigs. He longed to fill his stomach with the pods that the pigs were eating, but no one gave him anything.

"When he came to his senses, he said, 'How many of my father's hired servants have food to spare, and here I am starving to death! I will set out and go back to my father and say to him: Father, I have sinned against heaven and against you. I am no longer worthy to be called your son; make me like one of your hired servants.' So he got up and went to his father.

"But while he was still a long way off, his father saw him and was filled with compassion for him; he ran to his son, threw his arms around him and kissed him.

"The son said to him, 'Father, I have sinned against heaven and against you. I am no longer worthy to be called your son.'

"But the father said to his servants, 'Quick! Bring the best robe and put it on him. Put a ring on his finger and sandals on his feet. Bring the fattened calf and kill it. Let's have a feast and

celebrate. For this son of mine was dead and is alive again; he was lost and is found.' So they began to celebrate.

"Meanwhile, the older son was in the field. When he came near the house, he heard music and dancing. So he called one of the servants and asked him what was going on. 'Your brother has come,' he replied, 'and your father has killed the fattened calf because he has him back safe and sound.'

"The older brother became angry and refused to go in. So his father went out and pleaded with him. But he answered his father, 'Look! All these years I've been slaving for you and never disobeyed your orders. Yet you never gave me even a young goat so I could celebrate with my friends. But when this son of yours who has squandered your property with prostitutes comes home, you kill the fattened calf for him!'

"'My son,' the father said, 'you are always with me, and everything I have is yours. But we had to celebrate and be glad, because this brother of yours was dead and is alive again; he was lost and is found.'" (Luke 15:11-32 NIV)

Questions for Reflection

Where do you find yourself in this story? Why?

How are you like the wayward brother?

How are you like the older brother?

What is it about the father that captures your heart?

Does anything about him frustrate or disturb you?

When have you been truly celebrated? What did it feel like? What did it do in you?

Thoughts

There is something about being celebrated that strikes a chord deeply within all of us. It is something that we desperately long for. When we experience it, whether we realize it or not, we get a taste of the eternity we were created for. And when we don't, it throws us into a pit of doubt, insecurity, sadness, and despair.

Nowhere is that more evident than in the story of the Prodigal Son. It is a story about two sons, each of whom has a desperate longing to be celebrated. It is a story about leaving and returning. It is a story, on the one hand, about coming home and, on the other, about not fully realizing the home that you have. But, most of all, it is a story about the heart of a Father who longs for his two sons to know how unconditionally loved and deeply celebrated they are.

One had left home with his inheritance and returned with his tail between his legs, not feeling worthy of being loved or celebrated. Yet, upon his return, he gets both in extravagant measure. The other had stayed home, but still missed it somehow. Even though he had never left the Father's house, he still didn't understand the depths of the Father's love for him. You see, regardless of where our feet may (or may not) take us, we all have a deep longing to be celebrated — both the younger brothers of the world, as well as the older. And maybe particularly the older.

The older brother returns home from working in the fields and sees a party going on. Immediately his insecurities rise to the surface. "What is this celebration about? My younger brother? How is he worthy of a celebration? I'm the one who never left; this celebration should be for me."

The Father's words are priceless: "My son," affirming his sonship as well as the Father's affection, "you are always with me." Almost as if to say "*I love you and celebrate you every single day, don't you know that? In fact, everything I have is yours. If you only knew my deep love for you, and knew it to the core of your being. If you were only attentive enough each day to know how dear you are to me and how much love is in my heart for you. If you were only aware of how crazy about you I am and how much I celebrate you every day, then you would be secure enough in my love to celebrate the homecoming of your wayward brother. My celebration of him is not a threat to my celebration of you. You are my beloved! Know that truth to the depths of your being."*

Our need to be celebrated is so strong that we will have that need met one way or another — somehow, some way, somewhere. If we refuse to enter into the celebration God offers of us — either because it sounds too good to be true, or somehow not good enough — we will find a way and a crowd to celebrate us. Or we will chase after it for the rest of our lives. But the celebration we most deeply long for (in fact the celebration we were created for) lies only in the Father's celebration of us. And until we realize that, and live out of that reality, we will never find the rest and the peace we most deeply long for. So let us all turn the ear of our hearts toward God and listen to the words of affection and celebration he most deeply wants us to hear.

They might sound something like this: *Jim, my son, you are my Beloved. I know how much insecurity and doubt fills your heart and it makes me so sad. It hurts me deeply to see you doubting your value, your worth, and your calling. I know how much you compare yourself with others, and how much (in your mind anyway) you come up woefully short in that comparison. I long for you to know your own beauty, value, and worth. You have something to offer that no one else in all creation has ever had, or ever will have. You are a wonderfully unique expression of my love, care, and creativity, and it gives me such joy to see you be who I made you to be and give what I gave you to give.*

You are incomparable; beyond compare. You are of infinite worth. Come to me and allow me to celebrate over you daily. Allow me to convince you of my extravagant love. Allow me to convince you that you are worthy of being celebrated. And allow me to remind you that I celebrate you every minute of every day. You are mine!!! And I love you!!!

Pray
Pray that God would help you to know, and be fully convinced of, his great love for and celebration of you. Pray for others (specifically) in your life and world who need to hear his words as well.

Respond
In the space below, write a love letter to yourself from God. Fill it with all of the things he celebrates about you.

14 – Like treasure

Silence

Spend a few minutes in silence allowing your heart and mind to become still and calm. This will create good space within you for God to plant whatever treasure he desires in the soil of your soul today.

Read

"The kingdom of heaven is like treasure hidden in a field, which a man found and covered up. Then in his joy he goes and sells all that he has and buys that field." (Matthew 13:44 ESV)

Questions for Reflection

What do you truly treasure?

What makes that person or thing so significant to you?

How does what you treasure affect how you live?

What would it look like for Jesus to be your treasure?

Where might you find *treasure hidden* today?

Thoughts

What do I really think the *kingdom of heaven* is like? And how does what I really think the *kingdom of heaven* is like shape my life and my belief? I have a suspicion that if I really believed the *kingdom of heaven* was *like treasure*, I would live my life much differently. At least that was the case for those who found the *treasure*: the guy in the field, Zacchaeus, James and John, Peter and Andrew, and Paul. Something deeply significant happens in the heart of a person when they truly discover the beauty and the majesty, the breathtaking quality, of this *treasure*.

What comes to your mind when you hear the phrase *the kingdom of heaven*? And what comes to your mind when you think of *treasure*? What do you *treasure*? What is your *treasure*? It seems like a pretty significant question. In fact, both Matthew and Luke go as far as to tell us that "*where our treasure is, there our hearts will be also,*" so I guess it is something we should spend some time considering.

The more I think about it, once I am truly convinced that *life with God* (*the kingdom of heaven*) is like *treasure* — the most valuable, beautiful, captivating treasure I could ever hope to discover in my wildest dreams — it completely changes everything. My heart is completely and totally captured by its (His) beauty and I will do anything and give up anything and everything to possess it.

But the kingdom of heaven is not just like treasure, it's like *treasure hidden*. Now there's an interesting twist. Why in the world would God want this *treasure* to be *hidden*? The only answer I can come up with is that there must be some value in the seeking. And not only in the seeking for the very first time, but in the seeking each and every day after that as well. That means that the *why* of the hiddenness may not be quite as important as the *fact* that it is, indeed, *hidden*. For if it is *hidden* then that must be the very nature of this *treasure*. It is *hidden* and waiting to be found. And if that is the nature of this *treasure*, then we need to constantly be on the lookout for it. If there is buried *treasure* waiting to be found, we need to constantly be seeking and searching and digging to unearth it each minute of each and every day. Whether it be in a conversation, or a situation, or a circumstance, or a hardship, or a wound, or even in our time with him in Scripture. I must constantly be digging in search of the *treasure hidden in the field*. It is definitely there and is just waiting to be found. And when I begin to approach life in this way it will radically change everything. I will be completely *sold out* (like the man in the parable), giving up anything and everything to take possession of this immeasurably valuable treasure, in order to constantly make it my own.

Pray

Pray that God would convince you that life with him is indeed treasure. Ask him to give you eyes to see and a passion to seek that treasure today, wherever it may be found.

Respond

Spend some time writing about Jesus as hidden treasure. How and where will you look for him today?

15 – Little lamb, arise!

Silence

Spend a few minutes in silence allowing your heart and mind to come to rest. A wise saint once said that *silence is God's first language*. Therefore, if you desire to hear God's voice, it is most likely to happen in silence.

Read

And when Jesus had crossed again in the boat to the other side, a great crowd gathered about him, and he was beside the sea. Then came one of the rulers of the synagogue, Jairus by name, and seeing him, he fell at his feet and implored him earnestly, saying, "My little daughter is at the point of death. Come and lay your hands on her, so that she may be made well and live." And he went with him.

And a great crowd followed him and thronged about him. And there was a woman who had had a discharge of blood for twelve years, and who had suffered much under many physicians, and had spent all that she had, and was no better but rather grew worse. She had heard the reports about Jesus and came up behind him in the crowd and touched his garment. For she said, "If I touch even his garments, I will be made well." And immediately the flow of blood dried up, and she felt in her body that she was healed of her disease. And Jesus, perceiving in himself that power had gone out from him, immediately turned about in the crowd and said, "Who touched my garments?" And his disciples said to him, "You see the crowd pressing around you, and yet you say, 'Who touched me?'" And he looked around to see who had done it. But the woman, knowing what had happened to her, came in fear and trembling and fell down before him and told him the whole truth. And he said to her, "Daughter, your faith has made you well; go in peace, and be healed of your disease."

While he was still speaking, there came from the ruler's house some who said, "Your daughter is dead. Why trouble the Teacher any further?" But overhearing what they said, Jesus said to the ruler of the synagogue, "Do not fear, only believe." And he allowed no one to follow him except Peter and James and John the brother of James. They came to the house of the ruler of the synagogue, and Jesus saw a commotion, people weeping and wailing loudly. And when he had entered, he said to them, "Why are you making a commotion and weeping? The child is not dead but sleeping." And they laughed at him. But he put them all outside and took the child's father and mother and those who were with him and went in where the child was. Taking her by the hand he said to her, "Talitha cumi," which means, "Little girl, I say to you, arise." And immediately the girl got up and began walking (for she was twelve years of age), and they were immediately overcome with amazement. And he strictly charged them that no one should know this, and told them to give her something to eat. (Mark 5:21-43 NIV)

Questions for Reflection

Which of the people in this story can you relate to most? Why?

Where are the words *"Don't fear, only believe"* relevant in your life right now?

Is there any place in your life where you have just about lost hope? How does this story speak to that?

In what way(s) do the words *"Little one, arise"* speak to you right now?

Thoughts

One had been bleeding for twelve years, the other was just twelve years old. One had probably seen a good bit of her life come and go, the other, seemingly, had her whole life ahead of her. One was just a face in the crowd, the other was from a prominent family. One had most likely been abandoned by her family long ago as a result of a lengthy bout with an illness that rendered her untouchable (ceremonially unclean), the other had a loving father who would go to any length to give his little girl every opportunity available to be healed.

But while there were significant differences between the two, there were also many similarities. For both, life had taken a terribly wrong turn. Both had grasped for healing and wholeness from every available avenue. Both were now at the end of their rope — needy and desperate. Both had some sense that Jesus was their final real hope. And most importantly, though they had yet to realize it, both were dearly loved daughters of God.

After meeting one in the midst of a crowded street, Jesus now turns in the direction of the other. But it appears that, for this little one, he is too late. Jesus enters the house, taking a small group of family and friends with him. He goes into the room where the little girl is lying. He bends over, gently taking her hand, and whispers tenderly in her ear, *"Little girl, get up."* Or literally, in Aramaic, *"Little lamb, arise!"* His *little lamb* opens her eyes and gets up from her bed, as if simply waking from a peaceful night's sleep.

Desperation turns to celebration, mourning to dancing. The small band of onlookers is both amazed and overjoyed. Jesus turns to Jairus and his wife and, with a soft smile on his lips, says, with a wink, "Now… why don't you give her something to eat?"

Pray

What are your deepest fears these days? Give them to God in prayer. In return, ask him to give you a stronger belief in his care and a greater trust in his control.

Respond

Write some, in the space that follows, about whatever is going on in your heart and mind these days. What is he longing to whisper in your ear today?

16 – Born of the Spirit

Silence
Spend a few minutes in silence and allow your soul to come to stillness. Rest in his presence. Allow the stillness to awaken you to his voice and his Spirit.

Read
Now when he was in Jerusalem at the Passover Feast, many believed in his name when they saw the signs that he was doing. But Jesus on his part did not entrust himself to them, because he knew all people and needed no one to bear witness about man, for he himself knew what was in man.

Now there was a man of the Pharisees named Nicodemus, a ruler of the Jews. This man came to Jesus by night and said to him, "Rabbi, we know that you are a teacher come from God, for no one can do these signs that you do unless God is with him." Jesus answered him, "Truly, truly, I say to you, unless one is born again he cannot see the kingdom of God." Nicodemus said to him, "How can a man be born when he is old? Can he enter a second time into his mother's womb and be born?" Jesus answered, "Truly, truly, I say to you, unless one is born of water and the Spirit, he cannot enter the kingdom of God. That which is born of the flesh is flesh, and that which is born of the Spirit is spirit. Do not marvel that I said to you, 'You must be born again.' The wind blows where it wishes, and you hear its sound, but you do not know where it comes from or where it goes. So it is with everyone who is born of the Spirit." (John 2:23-3:8 ESV)

Questions for Reflection
What do you think about Nicodemus?

How are you like him? How are you not like him?

What was it about Nicodemus that made Jesus willing to "entrust himself" to him?

What was Jesus talking about when he said that we must be *born again*?

Why does you he later change the phrase to *born of the Spirit*?

How would you describe the Holy Spirit?

How did Jesus describe the Holy Spirit? What do you think about that?

Who is the Holy Spirit to you? What makes you say that?

Thoughts

There must have been something special about Nicodemus. Not so much because he was religious, or smart, or "learned" — it was something inside. After all, John just got finished telling us that Jesus refused to entrust himself to the people in Jerusalem because *he knew what was in a man.* Yet, when Nicodemus arrived at his doorstep in the middle of the night, Jesus welcomed him gladly. I wonder why? There must have been something special about the state of his heart. He must have been genuinely seeking truth. Jesus was always a pushover for someone genuinely seeking him. Just ask Jeremiah: "*You will seek me and find me when you seek me with all your heart. I will be found by you, declares the Lord.*" (Jeremiah 29:13-14)

So, on this particular evening, Nicodemus comes seeking. He comes because he realizes that Jesus is qualitatively different from anyone he has ever heard talk about God before. There is just something special in his words and in his spirit, something that Nicodemus can't quite describe, something he can't quite put his finger on. There is a life and a power and an authority in Jesus that he hasn't seen or heard before. And this *Spirit* makes something deep inside Nicodemus lean forward. It's like Jesus has touched something within him that he didn't even know was there.

As the conversation begins, Nicodemus is immediately challenged and amazed. Jesus has a whole new language, a whole new paradigm, a whole new way to look at and talk about the life of faith. This new picture that Jesus seems to be drawing is not so much about what you do — which has always been the cornerstone of the entire Pharisaical structure — but first about what God does in you. *"Truly, truly, I say to you, unless one is born again he cannot see the kingdom of God,"* Jesus says. This blows Nicodemus' mind. How is that even possible? A person can't go back into the womb and be born all over again. But Jesus is talking about *Spirit* and Nicodemus is thinking about *flesh*. For Nicodemus the physical world is his reality, but for Jesus the true reality is the world of the Spirit. The flesh is only fleeting and temporary. The Spirit-life is the real life. It is a life that cannot be manufactured, manipulated, or controlled. The work of the Spirit is all up to God. And in order to live this life with God, there must be a work of his Spirit done deep within us. His Spirit must be born in us and until that happens we are not really alive at all, but merely walking dead.

I would like to believe that, at some point, this work of God's Spirit happened in the heart of Nicodemus. In my heart of hearts I imagine that somewhere along the way he made the transition from flesh to Spirit. That somewhere along the way he crossed over from death to life. That somewhere along the way he moved from religion to relationship. That somewhere, somehow, some way that mysterious wind of God's Spirit blew through his life and totally captured his heart—and Nicodemus was, indeed, born again.

Pray
Pray for the movement of God's Spirit both within you and around you this day. Pray that something new would be born in you. Pray that those around you, those like Nicodemus, might be born again.

Respond
How, or where, do you sense the movement of God's Spirit in your life and world these days? Spend some time writing about it.

17 – Let down your nets for a catch

Silence

Spend a few minutes in silence allowing your heart and mind to become still and calm. If you are having difficulty concentrating, pick a meaningful word in your faith journey (like Jesus, or peace) and try repeating it over and over as a way of calling your mind and heart back to attention.

Read

One day as Jesus was standing by the Lake of Gennesaret, the people were crowding around him and listening to the word of God. He saw at the water's edge two boats, left there by the fishermen, who were washing their nets. He got into one of the boats, the one belonging to Simon, and asked him to put out a little from shore. Then he sat down and taught the people from the boat.

When he had finished speaking, he said to Simon, "Put out into deep water, and let down the nets for a catch."

Simon answered, "Master, we've worked hard all night and haven't caught anything. But because you say so, I will let down the nets."

When they had done so, they caught such a large number of fish that their nets began to break. So they signaled their partners in the other boat to come and help them, and they came and filled both boats so full that they began to sink.

When Simon Peter saw this, he fell at Jesus' knees and said, "Go away from me, Lord; I am a sinful man!" For he and all his companions were astonished at the catch of fish they had taken, and so were James and John, the sons of Zebedee, Simon's partners.

Then Jesus said to Simon, "Don't be afraid; from now on you will fish for people." So they pulled their boats up on shore, left everything and followed him. (Luke 5:1-11 NIV)

Questions for Reflection
How would you feel if you were Simon Peter and Jesus told you to *put out into deep water, and let down the nets for a catch* after you had just fished all night long with nothing to show for it?

Where in your life is Jesus asking you to *put out into deep water*?

When Peter says, *"Master, we've worked hard all night and haven't caught anything. But because you say so, I will let down the nets"* how do you think he is feeling? What is he thinking?

Where in your life do you feel like you've worked hard all night, but haven't caught anything?

If you had been in the boat with Jesus, now filled to overflowing with fish, what would your response have been?

What do you think of Simon Peter's response? Why do you think he said what he did?

What is God saying to you through this story today?

Thoughts

I get the sense that there is a particular inner posture God is calling me to these days, and it has everything in the world to do with these verses in Luke 5. It seems that there are currently quite a few places in my life where the words *worked all night* (or *toiled* in the ESV) *and haven't caught anything* seem to be appropriate. They are areas where I am trying my best to make something happen— something good even—and having little to no success, at least visibly anyway. But one day, as I was reading this passage, it hit me. Maybe I am trying like crazy to *achieve* something that can only be *received*. That seems to be one of the many treasures that these particular verses hold. Sometimes we work and sweat and toil, trying to *produce* an outcome that really can't be produced, but one that can only be *received*. And there is a certain posture required for each.

The posture of productivity is work, work, and more work. The problem is that, when it comes to the life of the Spirit, productivity isn't the point—fruitfulness is. And fruitfulness is never something I can produce or control, but something I can only make space for, care for, and tend. The end result is ultimately up to God. Therefore, the mistake I most often make is to take the posture of *productivity* for something that can only come about as a result of *fruitfulness*. And when I do that, ultimately, it ends in frustration.

Fruitfulness takes a different posture altogether. It requires a posture of openness, surrender, vulnerability, receptivity, and trust. That is what I have been seeing in these verses lately. The disciples had worked hard all night and had absolutely nothing to show for it. Then Jesus comes along and tells them to: "*Go back out there, except this time go to the deep water and simply let down your nets. Don't worry about the catch, I will take care of that. I'm more concerned with your posture right now. I'm more concerned with teaching you the difference between productivity and fruitfulness, because my Kingdom is all about fruitfulness. One day, instead of fishing for fish, you are going to be fishing for men. And when that day comes you need to learn the value of this posture of trust, openness, obedience, and receptivity. So go out into the deep water, even if that is a place where the fish are harder to find. That's the point. And when you get there let down your nets. That's it! Don't work and toil and sweat. Just let down your nets and wait on me. I will fill them, in my own time and in my own way. In fact, I am the only one who can fill them. And until you learn that truth you aren't going to be of much use to anyone."*

Pray
Just spend some time today being with Jesus in prayer. Just go out into the deep water and let down your nets. See what he fills them with.

Respond
Write down what went on in your heart and soul as you simply sat with Jesus. Did he fill your nets with anything? What?

18 – When you pray

Silence
Spend a few minutes in silence allowing your soul and spirit to come to stillness before God. This will prepare your heart to receive whatever he may have for you today.

Read
And when you pray, do not be like the hypocrites, for they love to pray standing in the synagogues and on the street corners to be seen by others. Truly I tell you, they have received their reward in full. But when you pray, go into your room, close the door and pray to your Father, who is unseen. Then your Father, who sees what is done in secret, will reward you. And when you pray, do not keep on babbling like pagans, for they think they will be heard because of their many words. Do not be like them, for your Father knows what you need before you ask him.

This, then, is how you should pray:
"Our Father in heaven,
hallowed be your name,
your kingdom come,
your will be done,
on earth as it is in heaven.
Give us today our daily bread.
And forgive us our debts,
as we also have forgiven our debtors.
And lead us not into temptation,
but deliver us from the evil one."

For if you forgive other people when they sin against you, your heavenly Father will also forgive you. But if you do not forgive others their sins, your Father will not forgive your sins. (Matthew 6:5-15 NIV)

Questions for Reflection

What is your definition of prayer?

What has been your experience of prayer thus far in your life?

What words would you use to describe your prayer life?

What words do you wish described your prayer life?

What is prayer for?

How does Jesus describe prayer?

What does Jesus say about prayer that surprises you?

What does he say about prayer that inspires you?

What does he say about prayer that invites you?

What does he say about prayer that challenges you?

Thoughts

I've always had a sneaking suspicion that there is much more to most things than meets the eye – prayer being one of them. For years I was under the impression that prayer consisted of closing your eyes, bowing your head, and talking to God. The images of prayer that I carried around in my heart and mind left much to be desired. Prayer was not an activity I was particularly drawn to or excited about. My guess is that this had much more to do with my definition of prayer than it did with the real practice of prayer.

It wasn't until much later in life that I began to see that maybe my definition of prayer was far too small and rigid. Prayer isn't so much about performing a duty as it is about building a wonderfully intimate relationship. Prayer is not simply throwing all the words I can muster at the unseen God, but it – at its very core – has always been about union with the God who lives within us. I think that's what Jesus is really getting at in Matthew 6:5-8 when he talks about prayer. He's trying to recapture the true meaning and practice of prayer, which is simply being with God.

It is as if God himself (through the words of Matthew 6) is saying: *Don't stand on street corners, don't babble on and on; prayer is much more intimate and personal than that. Instead, go into your closet – that space where true intimacy is possible – and shut the door. Leave everyone and everything else on the outside; I want it to be just you and me. I want us to be together in a place where I have your undivided attention. I have so much I want to say to you; so much of me that I want you to know. And this space and time is the place where that is most possible; the place where I can have the deepest desires of my heart fulfilled, which is just to be with you, my Beloved. Come inside where things are still and quiet and you can hear every whisper of my loving Spirit deep within your heart and soul. That's prayer.*

"Here's what I want you to do: Find a quiet, secluded place so you won't be tempted to role-play before God. Just be there as simply and honestly as you can manage. The focus will shift from you to God, and you will begin to sense his grace." (Matthew 6:6 The Message)

Pray
Use these verses in Matthew to guide your prayer time today. Find a quiet place, go into the room of your soul, and shut the door. Just spend some time being with God. Utter whatever words rise in your heart. Finish your time of prayer by saying the Lord's Prayer. Pray it slowly, pausing to reflect, or linger, as God leads.

Respond
Write a little about your definition, experience, and practice of prayer, as well as what you may have noticed during your time with Jesus today.

19 – Abiding

Silence
Spend a few minutes in silence. You should be getting used to this by now. Silence is the arena in which we are most likely to meet God. He typically doesn't speak loudly, but usually in a gentle whisper. Don't miss it.

Read
I am the true vine, and my Father is the vinedresser. Every branch in me that does not bear fruit he takes away, and every branch that does bear fruit he prunes, that it may bear more fruit. Already you are clean because of the word that I have spoken to you. Abide in me, and I in you. As the branch cannot bear fruit by itself, unless it abides in the vine, neither can you, unless you abide in me. I am the vine; you are the branches. Whoever abides in me and I in him, he it is that bears much fruit, for apart from me you can do nothing. If anyone does not abide in me he is thrown away like a branch and withers; and the branches are gathered, thrown into the fire, and burned. If you abide in me, and my words abide in you, ask whatever you wish, and it will be done for you. By this my Father is glorified, that you bear much fruit and so prove to be my disciples. As the Father has loved me, so have I loved you. Abide in my love. If you keep my commandments, you will abide in my love, just as I have kept my Father's commandments and abide in his love. These things I have spoken to you, that my joy may be in you, and that your joy may be full. (John 15:1-8 ESV)

Question for Reflection
What does the word *abide* mean to you?

What do you think Jesus meant when he said *abide in me*?

What does that look like?

Why do you think Jesus wants us to *abide in him*?

What does the picture of a vine and a branch communicate to you about the kind of relationship Jesus desires with you?

What other words, phrases, or images in this passage are significant to you? Why?

Thoughts

What kind of relationship do you think Jesus wants with you? The first words that pop into my head are words like obedient, reverent, and submissive—all of which are true. But here, in the upper room, the night before he is going to die on the cross, Jesus gives us a much different picture. It is a very intimate picture. He gives us the image of a vine and its branches. Almost as if to say, *"I know you have certain ideas floating around in your heads about what I want this relationship between you and me to be, but let me tell you, you can never imagine how deep and close and intimate I really want it to be. I want us to be closer than a vine and its branches."*

The main word he uses to describe this relationship is *abide*. He wants to *abide in us* and *us in him*. What do you think that really means? What are the characteristics of abiding in someone or something? If you look it up in the dictionary you will find that the word *abide* means to remain; continue; stay—which is exactly what the Greek word Jesus uses here (*meno*) means. It is a word that denotes constancy, intimacy, dependence, and continual connection. It is a deeply relational word.

As a matter of fact, this word didn't just show up out of the blue in John 15, it is also used in a number of other places in the gospels as well. Remember back in the first chapter of John, when Jesus asked the disciples what they were seeking? Their response was, "Where are you staying?" And then later it says, "And they stayed with him that day." That is the same word (*meno*). They literally said, "Where are you abiding?" And then, "And they abided with him that day."

It is also used in the Garden of Gethsemane (Matthew 26:38) — just a short time after the upper room — when Jesus is deeply troubled *to the point of death*. He asks them to *remain* and watch with him. That is the same word (*meno*) as well. What he is really asking is for them to *abide* with him; to stay deeply and relationally connected. But, unfortunately, the weary disciples are unable to abide with him due to their own weaknesses, and they fall asleep.

So what Jesus really wants from his disciples, both then and now, is not only a relationship of obedience, or reverence, or submission, but he wants much more than that. He wants a relationship of continual presence, constant connection, total dependence, and deep intimacy. In the words of Thomas Merton "he does not just want people living *for* him, or even *with* him, but he wants people living *in* him." And that is more than we could ever hope for or dream about. That is about as intimate and connected as you can get.

Pray

Practice abiding in Christ during your time of prayer today. Abide in him and realize that he is abiding in you. Do this for at least ten minutes. At the end ask him to teach you how to abide in him throughout the rest of the day.

Respond

Spend some time writing about abiding. What was it like in your prayer time? Draw a picture of abiding as an attempt to help you in your future efforts.

20 – Ordering our affections

Silence

Spend a few minutes in silence allowing your heart and soul to be still before God. Stillness allows us to be awake and attentive to God and to whatever he might want to say to us today.

Read

As Jesus and his disciples were on their way, he came to a village where a woman named Martha opened her home to him. She had a sister called Mary, who sat at the Lord's feet listening to what he said. But Martha was distracted by all the preparations that had to be made. She came to him and asked, "Lord, don't you care that my sister has left me to do the work by myself? Tell her to help me!"

"Martha, Martha," the Lord answered, "You are worried and upset about many things, but few things are needed – or indeed only one. Mary has chosen what is better, and it will not be taken away from her." (Luke 10:38-42 NIV)

Questions for Reflection

What words are used in the passage to describe Martha?

What does Jesus say to her?

How is Mary described?

What does Jesus say about her?

Which sister can you relate most to? Why?

What are you *worried* and *upset* about these days?

What would Jesus say to you about those things?

What would it look like in your life to choose what is *better*?

How can you choose the *one thing* rather than the *many things*?

Thoughts

One of the most important things in all of the spiritual life, the saints tell us, is learning to order our affections. In fact, Saint Ignatius tells us that one of the biggest obstacles and/or hindrances to living in continuous union with God is disordered affections.

There is a created order to all things — an intentional design. When that created order is followed, a coherent life is the result. But whenever that created order is not adhered to, there is chaos. That's why Jesus, when he was asked by "an expert in the law" in Matthew 22 which commandment was the greatest, immediately responds: *"Love the Lord your God with all your heart and with all your soul and with all your mind. This is the first and greatest commandment. And the second is like it: love your neighbor as yourself. All the Law and the Prophets hang on these two commandments."* For there is even (and most particularly) a created order to our *loves*. Unless we love God with all of our being *first*, we can never truly love anyone or anything else with the love that we were created to love them with. As Henri Nouwen put it years ago, "The second love can only be a reflection of the first." Therefore, when we love anyone or anything more than we love God, we have gone against the created order, which produces all kinds of disorder and chaos.

I think that's what Jesus was getting at in Luke 10 with Mary and Martha. Martha was *distracted*. She had allowed the long list of things that "had to be done" to get in the way of the most important thing. The urgent had taken precedence over the important. When she came to Jesus and aired her complaint, he gently reminded her of this truth: *"Martha, Martha, you are worried and upset about many things, but few things are needed — or indeed only one."* Sometimes our zeal to get things done *for* Jesus keeps us from recognizing the necessity of being *with* Jesus *first*. That is the created order. Thus, the order of our affections is a very important part of the equation.

Mary had it right. When Jesus walked into the room nothing else mattered. The most important thing in the world was simply finding her way to his feet and listening to what he had to say. There was a time for work, but this was the time for worship. Her affection for Jesus overruled her affection for everything else. Jesus was her first and truest affection. Jesus was her *one thing*. For if Jesus is your first and truest affection, then the *many things* of this life seem to fall in order behind him. Our lives become *centered on* and *rooted in* the love of Jesus.

Unfortunately *disordered affections* can be very difficult to recognize because the things that end up occupying most of our time and our energy (which is a very good way to tell what's really at the center of our lives) are often very *good things*: job, work, service, reputation, achievements, accomplishments, ministry, hobbies, exercise, and even family activities. But *anything* that takes precedence over our affection for him has become the center of our lives. And that is a spot that was designed only for Him to occupy.

So the question becomes: *What occupies most of my time, energy, and focus these days?* What has my heart? What is my *one thing* right now? And what does it look like for Jesus to be my first and truest affection? The answer to these questions can give us a pretty good idea about whether our lives, and our affections, are properly ordered.

Pray
Pray that God would reveal your disordered affections to you.

Respond

Spend some time thinking about, and writing about, your disordered affections. How is that currently taking shape in your life? What is the impact of these disordered affections? What would it look like for God to be your first and truest affection?

21 – Do you see anything?

Silence

Spend a few minutes in silence allowing your heart and soul to be still before God. Rest in his presence. Allow the stillness to awaken you to his Voice and his Spirit.

Read

They came to Bethsaida, and some people brought a blind man and begged Jesus to touch him. He took the blind man by the hand and led him outside the village. When he had spit on the man's eyes and put his hands on him, Jesus asked, "Do you see anything?"

He looked up and said, "I see people; they look like trees walking around."

Once more Jesus put his hands on the man's eyes. Then his eyes were opened, his sight was restored, and he saw everything clearly. Jesus sent him home, saying, "Don't even go into the village." (Mark 8:22-26 NIV)

Questions for Reflection

As you step into this story, what captures your attention? Why?

If you had been one of the disciples, what would you have been thinking?

If you were the blind man, what would you have been thinking?

Why do you think Jesus touched the man twice to heal his blindness?

How are you seeing Jesus in stages these days?

What about him has become clearer to you since we began this journey?

Thoughts

Do you see anything? What a great question. Notice, at this point at least, what Jesus didn't ask. He didn't ask, "Do you see everything clearly?" I wonder why? Maybe it's because that wasn't the purpose of the first touch.

Life is absolutely full of decisions that have to be made and most of the time these decisions are anything but clear — at least to me anyway. It seems like I'm constantly in the midst of seeking God's direction in one aspect of life or another. And, for the most part, clarity seems to come rather slowly, if at all. I would love for things to become clear all at once, but maybe that's not exactly what Jesus wants for me, or not exactly what's going to accomplish the purposes he wants to accomplish in me. While I want the question to be, "Do you see everything clearly?" because absolute clarity is what I'm looking for and hoping for most of the time, maybe he wants the question to be,

"Do you see anything?" Because maybe he wants to leave enough uncertainty so that it makes me completely rely on him. Richard Rohr once said that faith is *a kind of knowing that is patient with not knowing.* Maybe God wants to leave enough *not knowing* so that I actually have to trust in his infinite love and care, rather than my own ability to chart my path and determine my course.

So, in the absence of complete clarity, he leaves me with the question, "Do you see anything?" And it's a pretty great question when you *really* hear it and try to answer it. I know I might not be able to see everything clearly right now, but what, exactly, can I see? Even if my answer is something like, *"I see people; they look like trees walking around,"* it is still a really great question because trying to answer it has begun a process, which is exactly what Jesus seems to be trying to teach the disciples in the first place — *that seeing clearly is almost always a process.* It doesn't all happen on the first touch. If it did we would have no further need for subsequent touches.

For instance, immediately after the disciples had just seen Jesus feed two different enormous groups of people with just a few loaves and a couple of fish they got into a boat and started worrying about having no bread. Are you kidding me? They were seeing dimly to say the least, but at least they were seeing; especially when he called it to their attention. And now, to illustrate his point, he heals a blind man in stages. Incredible!

So there must be value in the process, or we would all be able to see everything on the first touch, right? Because when we focus on the question, "Do you see anything?" it allows us to still be in that process. It requires us to be dependent on him, to continue to seek him. Trying to answer that question allows us to lean into an answer in a much slower, much more formative way. It's almost as if

God is saying *"If I give you the answer then you will stop seeking me, and the seeking is really what I'm after."*

So maybe the best thing we can do, until complete clarity comes (if it ever does), is to ask ourselves, "What do I see?" And, as I have asked myself that question, I have begun to realize (or *see*) a few things. *I see that God is at work. I see that people are hungry for him. I see that he is continually working to lead and guide us if we will just pay attention. I see that I still need clarity on a few things in particular, but that clarity usually comes over time, rather than all at once. I see that, although I cannot see everything clearly, I can see something. And that something is a really good thing.*

O Jesus, touch my eyes again and again until I am able to *see everything clearly.* And, in the meantime, help me to trust your tender love and care, and be attentive to *what I can see*.

Pray
Pray that Jesus would touch your eyes today, as well as the eyes of those around you. Pray that he would allow you to recognize what you *can see*. And pray that he would continually touch you with his healing hands, allowing you to *see* more clearly (with his eyes) every day.

Respond
Make a list of what you *do see*.

22 – She has done a beautiful thing

Silence

Spend some time in silence allowing your heart and soul to come to rest. Just be fully present to God and to whatever he might want to do or say. Your undivided attention is a gift to him. It is like perfume on his head.

Read

While he was in Bethany, reclining at the table in the home of Simon the Leper, a woman came with an alabaster jar of very expensive perfume, made of pure nard. She broke the jar and poured the perfume on his head.

Some of those present were saying indignantly to one another, "Why this waste of perfume? It could have been sold for more than a year's wages and the money given to the poor." And they rebuked her harshly.

"Leave her alone," said Jesus. "Why are you bothering her? She has done a beautiful thing to me. The poor you will always have with you, and you can help them any time you want. But you will not always have me. She did what she could. She poured perfume on my body beforehand to prepare for my burial. Truly I tell you, wherever the gospel is preached throughout the world, what she has done will also be told, in memory of her." (Mark 14:3-9 NIV)

Questions for Reflection

What wells up within you as you read this story?

What words or phrases speak deeply to you? Why?

Who do you relate to most in this story? Why?

How do you feel when you give something extravagantly to someone you love?

How does it feel to receive love this extravagant?

What do you have that you want to pour out on Jesus today?

Thoughts

She'd had *it* most of her life. Her father gave it to her when she was just a little girl, and thus, it was precious to her. It was precious not merely because it was extremely valuable, but because it was all she had left of him. She had intended to save it for the day of her wedding, to give as a gift of extravagant love to her Beloved. That was before she met Jesus. When she met him it changed everything. He had completely captured her heart. Now the question wasn't if she would give it to him, but how and when. For some reason this felt like the right time.

She pulled the jar down off the shelf in her room, the glass shimmering in the candlelight. She had often looked at it, marveling how anything could be so beautiful — and that was just the outside. What was inside was even better. It was by far the most delightful fragrance she had ever smelled. And it should be, it was made of pure nard. She could work an entire year and still not have enough money to buy another jar. And she couldn't wait to give it all to Jesus.

She entered the room, smiling from ear to ear, tears of joy rolling down her cheeks. She broke the jar, pouring the entirety of its contents — pure and undiluted — on his head. An aroma sweeter than you could ever dream about in your wildest dreams filled the room. And it was even sweeter to Jesus, for she was not just pouring out her perfume, but her heart — which he gladly received every drop of. It was her "I love you" to the lover of her soul.

Jesus, head back, eyes closed, tears of gratitude rolling down his cheeks, was basking in this intimate moment when, suddenly, he was interrupted by jeers and rebukes. *"Why this waste of perfume?"* they harshly complained, *"It could have been sold for more than a year's wages and the money given to the poor."* Isn't it funny how an act of love by one can create so much insecurity in others? Deep inside they must have known what a beautiful thing they had just witnessed, but since they hadn't thought of it themselves they decided to hurl criticism at her instead.

Jesus would have none of it. *"Leave her alone,"* he said. *"Why are you bothering her? She has done a beautiful thing to me. She did what she could. I tell you the truth, wherever the gospel is preached throughout the world, what she has done will also be told, in memory of her."*

Each of us has something beautiful to give. It is something that is breathed into us when we are created. It is something that is woven into the very fabric of our being by the God who made us. It is something unique and wonderful that has been given to us and to no other. It is our own jar of pure nard, our own uniquely fragrant giftedness that our Father gave us before we ever came into being, given specifically to be used for his glory and delight.

And when we discover exactly what our particular perfume is, and we use that perfume in service to and love for him, it has a qualitative effect on everyone around us. It even has a qualitative effect on us — it reproduces itself within us somehow, even as it is given away. Our job is to discover what it is that he has put within us to give and then to give it. Notice that Jesus says about the woman, *"She did what she could."* She knew what she had to give (and what she didn't have to give) and gave it freely and fully, without diluting or distorting it. May it be the same for each of us. May we discover that fragrant perfume we have been given and may we figure out how and when and where to give it. And when we do, it will surely leave Jesus saying, "She/he has done a beautiful thing to me."

Pray

Pray that God would show you what your "pure nard" is. It was given to you so that you could pour it on the head of Jesus.

Respond

Write down the gifts that God has given to you — gifts given for the purpose of pouring them out for his glory and delight. Ask a few others what they think your "perfume" is. Think of a couple of people you are close to and go tell them what you see in them that God has breathed into them for his glory and delight.

23 – You give them something to eat

Silence

Spend a few minutes in silence allowing your heart and soul to be still before God. Rest in his presence. Allow the stillness to awaken you to his Voice and his Spirit.

Read

The apostles gathered around Jesus and reported to him all they had done and taught. Then, because so many people were coming and going that they did not even have a chance to eat, he said to them, "Come with me by yourselves to a quiet place and get some rest."

So they went away by themselves in a boat to a solitary place. But many who saw them leaving recognized them and ran on foot from all the towns and got there ahead of them. When Jesus landed and saw a large crowd, he had compassion on them, because they were like sheep without a shepherd. So he began teaching them many things.

By this time it was late in the day, so his disciples came to him. "This is a remote place," they said, "and it's already very late. Send the people away so that they can go to the surrounding countryside and villages and buy themselves something to eat."

But he answered, "You give them something to eat."

They said to him, "That would take more than half a year's wages! Are we to go and spend that much on bread and give it to them to eat?"

"How many loaves do you have?" he asked. "Go and see."

When they found out, they said, "Five — and two fish."

Then Jesus directed them to have all the people sit down in groups on the green grass. So they sat down in groups of hundreds and fifties. Taking the five loaves and the two fish and looking up to heaven, he gave thanks and broke the loaves. Then he gave them to his disciples to distribute to the people. He also divided the two fish among them all. They all ate and were satisfied, and the disciples picked up twelve basketfuls of broken pieces of bread and fish. The number of the men who had eaten was five thousand. (Mark 6:30-44 NIV)

Questions for Reflection

What about this story speaks most to your current story?

As you walk with Jesus through this story, what do you notice about him? What captures you?

Why do you think he gave the food to the disciples to give to the people?

Where do you think Jesus was as the disciples were passing out the food?

If you were someone in the hungry crowd who had just been fed, what would you wonder about Jesus?

As the disciples picked up the broken pieces do you think that they were surprised that there was a basket of food leftover for each of them?

Thoughts

You give them something to eat. It seems that a significant amount of doing ministry involves figuring out what you've got—even if it feels like just *five loaves of bread and two fish*—and then figuring out how to give it and who to give it to. As we said in the last chapter, God gave you something wonderfully unique and specific, something that only you can give. It may feel like only five loaves and two fish to you, but, in his hands, it is more than enough to satisfy all and still have some left over. *You give them something to eat, because I gave you something very specific that only you can give. First of all, give it to me, and then I will give it back to you in abundance. Only then will you have enough to give it to them, whoever your "them" may be. And in the giving of it to them you will find that there is enough to feed you as well.* Pretty incredible!

There is one other small thing to notice however. And it really is not small at all. Once we are willing enough and courageous enough to give Jesus our little loaves and fish, he does something really amazing with it. Amazing and frightening all at the same time. He *takes* it, then he *blesses* it, then he *breaks* it, and then he *gives* it. Now all of that sounds pretty great, except the breaking part. Because, it seems, in Jesus' economy, we can't be multiplied enough to be given, we can only be broken enough to be given. It is in the breaking that the multiplying seems to occur. It is in the breaking that the abundance seems to come about. As it will be for each of us.

If we really want to have something of depth and substance to give, it will usually involve some sort of breaking. The funny thing is when we feel the most broken in our lives, that is usually the time when we feel least able to give, or the time when we feel like we have the least to offer, but just the opposite is true. It is when we are broken that we are actually most able to fruitfully give ourselves. Because somehow, in the brokenness, it has stopped being about us and our ability to multiply ourselves, and has begun being about God and his ability to multiply our little loaves and fish with his strong and tender hands.

Pray
Ask God to whom he wants you to give yourself for his sake today.

Respond
Does the word *taken, blessed, broken,* or *given* seem most significant to you these days? Which best describes your life? Your ministry? What makes you say that?

24 – Rest

Silence

Spend a few minutes in silence allowing your heart and soul to be still before God. Rest in his presence. Allow the stillness to awaken you to his Voice and his Spirit.

Read

"Are you tired? Worn out? Burned out on religion? Come to me. Get away with me and you'll recover your life. I'll show you how to take a real rest. Walk with me and work with me — watch how I do it. Learn the unforced rhythms of grace. I won't lay anything heavy or ill-fitting on you. Keep company with me and you'll learn to live freely and lightly." (Matthew 11:28-30, The Message)

Questions for Reflection

Do you find it odd that one of the things Jesus wants most for you is rest? Why do you think that is?

How do you define the word *rest*?

How do you think God defines it?

Why does rest seem so important to God?

Is it important to you?

Are you able to truly rest? Why or why not?

What makes your heart and soul feel truly rested?

Thoughts

"Are you too exhausted to run and too scared to rest?" It was just one sentence in the middle of a novel I was reading years ago (*At Home in Mitford* by Jan Karon), but it stopped me in my tracks. An older mentor was having a conversation with a young pastor about his busy life and his dry and weary soul, and this was the question he asked him. And what a question! It was a question that cut right to my heart and soul, because somehow I knew that it was for me.

Why in the world would I be too scared to rest? Does it have something to do with the fact that I feel like I have to earn everything? Does it have something to do with the fact that my entire sense of value and worth (my identity) is completely tied up in what I do? Thus, if I am not doing anything of value, then I am not worth anything. Does it have something to do with my need to be needed? Have I somehow tried to convince my world—and myself—that I am indispensable? That if I am not present and active in the running of things, they would simply fall apart? And would I, in some incredibly warped and twisted way, secretly want them to fall apart? Or does it have something to do with my need for control? And the fact that as long as I have my hands in *it*, whatever *it* may be, then, and only then, can I trust that things will be done well?

Do you see what all of these questions have in common? Fear. We might try to dress them up in far more noble clothes, but they are just clever disguises. At the root of our inability, or unwillingness, to rest is fear.

Why is rest so important anyway? Isn't it really just being lazy and selfish? Why should I rest? I guess the best reason is because rest is important to God. In fact it is so important to God that he wove it into the very fabric of creation. Rest is a part of the rhythm that comes straight from his inner being. God spent six days creating, dreaming things into being, working, if you will, and then he rested. And he calls us, those made in his image, to do the same. Which means that when we choose not to rest, we working against the very image of God within us.

This rest that we are talking about is physical, yes, but it is so much more than that. It is also deeply spiritual. It is rest for our bodies *and* rest for our hearts and souls. It is time when we unplug from everything else, so that we might fully plug into him. It is time that is meant to renew and restore and refresh us to do the work God has given us to do, so we may do it far more fruitfully. It is part of the natural order, just like inhaling and exhaling. We were not created in a way that we can live in constant exhale. But that is exactly what so many of us try to do. And when we do that, we do it to our, and ultimately God's, detriment.

Here in Matthew, Jesus invites us to come to him and truly rest. To let go of everything else — all of our worries, our burdens, and our cares — and trust in his continual love and care. Let us take him up on his invitation and not allow our fears to get the better of us.

Pray
Just take a few minutes and accept Jesus' invitation. Rest in his embrace.

Respond
Write about your thoughts and feelings on rest.

25 – Weeping and kissing

Silence

Spend a few minutes in silence before God and allow your heart and mind to become still and calm. Try to drop all agendas and expectations and just be open to him and whatever he might want to do or say.

Read

When one of the Pharisees invited Jesus to have dinner with him, he went to the Pharisee's house and reclined at the table. A woman in that town who lived a sinful life learned that Jesus was eating at the Pharisee's house, so she came there with an alabaster jar of perfume. As she stood behind him at his feet weeping, she began to wet his feet with her tears. Then she wiped them with her hair, kissed them and poured perfume on them.

When the Pharisee who had invited him saw this, he said to himself, "If this man were a prophet, he would know who is touching him and what kind of woman she is – that she is a sinner."

Jesus answered him, "Simon, I have something to tell you."

"Tell me, teacher," he said.

"Two people owed money to a certain moneylender. One owed him five hundred denarii, and the other fifty. Neither of them had the money to pay him back, so he forgave the debts of both. Now which of them will love him more?"

Simon replied, "I suppose the one who had the bigger debt forgiven."

"You have judged correctly," Jesus said.

Then he turned toward the woman and said to Simon, "Do you see this woman? I came into your house. You did not give me any water for my feet, but she wet my feet with her tears and wiped them with her hair. You did not give me a kiss, but this

woman, from the time I entered, has not stopped kissing my feet.
You did not put oil on my head, but she has poured perfume on
my feet. Therefore, I tell you, her many sins have been
forgiven – as her great love has shown. But whoever has been
forgiven little loves little."

Then Jesus said to her, "Your sins are forgiven."

The other guests began to say among themselves, "Who is
this who even forgives sins?"

Jesus said to the woman, "Your faith has saved you; go in
peace." (Luke 7:36-50 NIV)

Questions for Reflection
Who can you relate to most in this story? Why?

How are you like the woman?

How are you like the Pharisee?

What things in your life cause you to weep right now?

How does it feel to know that you have been forgiven?

Do you feel like you have been forgiven much or little?

What is your response to that forgiveness?

Thoughts

She is not named, but everyone seemed to know who she was. In fact, she had quite a reputation in town. It would seem that her reputation had even become her identity. That is until she met Jesus. We're not told exactly when or how that happened, but somewhere along the line these two had met before, and it had changed everything about her.

Now here she is, on this particular evening, entering a house she had no business entering. A woman "like her" just didn't barge into the house of a Pharisee, especially when he was entertaining. He had invited Jesus to dine with him and a bunch of his Pharisee buddies, so they could all get an up close look at the one everyone was talking about. Whether it was curiosity or hostility that inspired the invitation we are not sure, although we can probably guess. All we are sure of is that he had invited Jesus to his house, and that he and his guests were reclining at the table.

It is into the midst of this "dinner party" that *she* comes, uninvited and uncaring that she is uninvited. She doesn't care about protocol. She doesn't care about political correctness. She doesn't care what anyone thinks or says. All she cares about is getting to the feet of her beloved Jesus. She only has eyes for him. So she enters the room and doesn't look back, making a beeline straight for his feet. And when she gets to him she does an amazing thing: *she stands behind him at his feet weeping, and begins to wet his feet with her tears. Then she wipes them with her hair, kisses them and pours perfume on them.* Did you catch that? She is *weeping* and she is *kissing*—sorrow and affection. Two things that seem completely contrary, but are actually inseparable. It is the gospel brought to life—two things that always must be connected in this life of faith. It cannot be just one or the other, it must always be both.

There is always a *weeping* that is such a necessary part of the picture. It involves a deep recognition of our utter sinfulness, brokenness, helplessness, and desperation. It is what happens within us when we come face to face with the absolute horror of our sin, which crucified Christ. But this *weeping* is much more than simply crying; it is an activity that is redemptive. It involves a deep recognition, a deep admission, and a deep healing. These are not normal tears, they come from somewhere way down inside; from that place of godly sorrow that Paul talks about in 2 Corinthians 7:10. The godly sorrow that leads to repentance. But as necessary as the *weeping* is, we can't stop there. There is more.

That's where the *kissing* comes in. For not only did this woman *weep*, she also *kissed*. As a matter of fact, the literal translation of the Greek is that she *kissed much*. She smothered him with kisses. She could not stop kissing him. She just went on and on. That's why Jesus says, *"This woman, from the time I entered, has not stopped kissing my feet."* His love for her had completely captured her heart. It had kindled an uncontrollable affection deep within her that simply could not be contained. She could not stop even if she wanted to, so smitten with love for him was she.

This is the part we usually miss as we wallow around in our sinfulness. But it is the part that we can't afford to miss because it is the beauty of the gospel. We cannot stop at weeping, we must always be *kissing* him as well—and *kissing* him much at that. Which begs the question: are we completely captured by his love? Does a deep affection for him well up from the core of our being? Are we showering him with our kisses? Are we falling more and more deeply in love with him each and every day?

Pray

Weep over your sin before God in prayer today. Claim his forgiveness and his cleansing. It will make room within you for his love. Now lavish him with kisses for his great love and forgiveness. Love him much.

Respond

Write some about where weeping is going on in your life and heart right now. And then write some about where kissing is going on within you these days.

26 – It is finished

Silence

Spend a few minutes in silence preparing your heart for whatever God might have for you today.

Read

After this, Jesus, knowing that all was now finished, said (to fulfill the Scripture), "I thirst." A jar full of sour wine stood there, so they put a sponge full of the sour wine on a hyssop branch and held it to his mouth. When Jesus had received the sour wine, he said, "It is finished," and he bowed his head and gave up his spirit. (John 19:28-30 ESV)

Questions for Reflection

When you hear the words *"It is finished"* what does it do within you?

What is finished?

What does it mean for you to live like *"It is finished"*?

What is your greatest struggle in letting *it be finished*?

What does *"It is finished"* take away from you?

What does it give you?

Thoughts

"It is finished." Jesus' final words. And what incredible words they are! *"It is finished"* means that the entire reason Jesus came to earth has been fulfilled — his mission has been accomplished. There is nothing else that needs to be done. Jesus has taken care of it all. All of our sin has been paid for in its entirety: past, present, and future. All of our punishment, every single ounce, has been placed upon him at the cross. *"It is finished"* means that we are totally justified — clean, holy, and free. *"It is finished"* means that our sin is taken away, we may go in peace.

But *"It is finished"* also means so much more than that. Because *"It is finished"* is not just about what God has taken away, but also about what he has given us. Jesus not only takes all of our mess — our sin, our brokenness, our death — upon himself, but he also gives us all that is his to give. He gives us his righteousness, he gives us his holiness, and he gives us his peace. He also gives us all of the love and affection of the Father. He gives us his inheritance, he gives us his place in the family of God, and he gives us the right to become God's beloved sons and daughters. So *"It is finished"* not only says "you may go, your sin is taken away," but it also says, "you may come and enjoy all of the intimacy of the Godhead." Because of the cross, this is now what God says to us: *My child, my delight, the joy of my heart, I wish you knew yourself the way I know you. I wish you saw yourself the way that I see you. And I wish that, deep down in your heart, you knew the truth that, because of the cross, all I have is yours and all you have is mine. Knowing this one truth at your very core will change everything about you. Now, all of my love is yours, all of my affection is yours, and all of my delight is yours. In fact, you have completely captured my heart. And not only that, but you also have all of my righteousness, all of my holiness, and all of my purity. Everything I have belongs to you.*

And all that you have is mine. Your joys are mine and your wounds are mine, your strengths are mine and your weaknesses are mine, your gifts are mine and your inadequacies are mine; so are your insecurities, your anxieties, your fears, your struggles, your burdens, yes, and even your sin – all mine. Come to me, my child, with all that you are, and let me give you all that I am in return. Be mine.

Pray

Give thanks to Jesus for his cross. Thank him for all that he has taken away and for all that he has given in return.

Respond

Have a conversation with Jesus, as he hangs on the cross. What do you want to say to him? What do you think he wants to say to you? Hear him utter the words, "*It is finished.*" How do those words make you feel?

27 – Risen wounds

Silence

Spend a few minutes in silence allowing your heart and mind to become still and calm. This stillness will create fruitful space within you to be able to hear God's word for you today.

Read

On the evening of that first day of the week, when the disciples were together, with the doors locked for fear of the Jewish leaders, Jesus came and stood among them and said, "Peace be with you!" After he said this, he showed them his hands and side. The disciples were overjoyed when they saw the Lord. (John 20:19-20 NIV)

Questions for Reflection

What do you think it would've been like to see the resurrected Jesus?

Where are the "locked doors of fear" within you? What would it look like for the risen Jesus to enter into those?

Where in your life do you need to hear the words *"Peace be with you"*?

When you look at Jesus' hands and side (now risen) what does it do within you?

What wounds need to be *risen* in your life?

How can those wounds become a source of life and healing to others?

Thoughts

You just never knew when or where he might show up next. One minute you would be walking down a road, or fishing on the sea, or locked in a room, and then suddenly, out of nowhere, there he was standing right next to you. There was just something wild and unpredictable about him. You never knew where he might show up next. Don't you love that? He is a God you can't control or manipulate, one who is wild and free. It seems like after the resurrection you just never knew quite what to expect; Jesus was likely to show up at any time and in any place. And because of that, there was a constant sense of excitement, amazement, and anticipation in the air.

On this particular evening we are told that *the disciples were together, with the doors locked for fear of the Jewish leaders* when, all of the sudden, *Jesus came and stood among them.* And into the midst of their fearful and hiding hearts he speaks the words, *"Peace be with you."* Then he shows them his hands and side and *the disciples are overjoyed.*

There are so many things I like about this passage; so many things I love about what Jesus was up to in the hearts (and the faith) of his friends. First of all, I love that he came *through* their locked doors and *into* the midst of their deepest fears. Those two obstacles didn't stop him. As a matter of fact, they didn't even seem to slow him down. He doesn't judge, he doesn't chide, he doesn't lecture—he just comes.

I know that my fears constantly cause me to hide behind the locked doors of my life. My fear of failure can make me hide behind the locked doors of inadequacy, making sure that I only operate in the safety zone of my gifts and never attempt anything where there might be risk or uncertainty involved. My fear of rejection can cause me to live behind the locked doors of familiarity, making sure that I only give myself to those with whom I feel safe and comfortable. And my fear of being unlovable can cause me to hide behind the locked doors of distance and introversion, fearing that if anyone really got to know me then they would see how unlovable I really am. But Jesus does not let these fears and locked doors keep him from coming and casting out all of my fears with his perfect love. (1 John 4:19)

I also love that, in the midst of these fears and locked doors, he speaks words of peace. What Jesus is really talking about here is the Hebrew idea of *shalom*. Few words in all of the bible are as rich as this one little word. As a matter of fact, the translations of this word are varied and numerous—trying, in vain, to capture the fullness of the idea it is meant to communicate. The most common translation we have is *peace*, but that does not begin to go far enough. Therefore, *shalom* is also translated *prosperity, tranquility, well-being, safety*, and *security*. Maybe the best word we have in the English language that even comes close to capturing the true essence of *shalom* is the word *wholeness*. Because at its core *shalom* is about experiencing the creation intent of God. *Shalom* is life as God intended it to be—life before sin and brokenness, life before locked doors and hiding in fear. *Shalom* is finding our way back into the Garden where we were able to enjoy and experience God in his fullness as we "walk with him in the cool of the day." It is what our souls are really and truly longing for—deep communion and connection and intimacy with our God. And, as the disciples hide in this locked room, this is what Jesus offers them.

Finally, I love that Jesus still bore his wounds in his resurrected body. And that as he stood among his friends, who all had deep wounds of their own, he showed his *risen wounds* to them as a source of life and hope. Hope that healing and wholeness is possible. Hope that our wounds too can be resurrected and converted into sources of life and hope for others, if we are just willing to share them. For it is by his wounds (now risen) that we have been healed. (Isaiah 53:5)

Pray
Spend some time with God this day offering him all of your wounds. Ask him for healing and wholeness. Ask him for *shalom*. Ask him to show you today who needs to see your risen wounds in order to find healing and wholeness of their own.

Respond
Write about the ways that God has healed your wounds, as well as the places that are still in need of healing. Also, write down the names of people in your life with whom he might want you to share these risen wounds as a source of life and hope.

28 – Do you truly love me?

Silence

Spend a few minutes in silence preparing your heart for whatever God might have for you today. Give him your full attention.

Read

When they had finished eating, Jesus said to Simon Peter, "Simon son of John, do you love me more than these?"

"Yes, Lord," he said, "you know that I love you."

Jesus said, "Feed my lambs."

Again Jesus said, "Simon son of John, do you love me?"

He answered, "Yes, Lord, you know that I love you."

Jesus said, "Take care of my sheep."

The third time he said to him, "Simon son of John, do you love me?"

Peter was hurt because Jesus asked him the third time, "Do you love me?" He said, "Lord, you know all things; you know that I love you."

Jesus said, "Feed my sheep. Very truly I tell you, when you were younger you dressed yourself and went where you wanted; but when you are old you will stretch out your hands, and someone else will dress you and lead you where you do not want to go." Jesus said this to indicate the kind of death by which Peter would glorify God. Then he said to him, "Follow me!"
(John 21:15-19 NIV)

Questions for Reflection

Do you truly love him more than these?

What is your *"these?"*

What are the most frequent rivals to your love of Jesus?

Are you feeding his lambs or feeding on his lambs? How?

Where is God asking you to go *where you would rather not go?*

Who sets the direction and agenda for your days? For your life?

What would it look like to really follow Jesus?

Thoughts

They are walking down the shoreline in the early
morning sun. It had been days since that fateful night. It
is just the two of them, with John following well behind.
Jesus had something he wanted to ask his friend, and he
didn't want to put him on the spot by asking in front of the
others. It was an intimate question and it called for an
intimate setting.

Peter could sense something was coming, but didn't
quite know what. There was still a good bit of shame and
disappointment lingering deep within his soul as he
replayed, over and over again, that dreaded scene from the
night of Jesus' arrest. Peter had *denied* him, three times.
He had *denied* his master, his teacher, and his best friend.
He had done the very thing he swore just hours before that

he would never do. It was still so fresh, so painful, so haunting, so humiliating.

As they walk, Jesus senses that there is a lot below the surface of his friend's silence. A deep wrestling is going on. So he turns to Peter and asks the question, *"Simon son of John, do you truly love me more than these?"* In fact, three times Jesus asks it, and three times Peter answers—three chances to confess that which he had denied only days earlier. It is such a sweet picture of grace and intention and restoration, even though Peter doesn't fully realize what is going on. Jesus is offering him a second chance. Jesus is saying: *Peter, I love you more than life itself. I dreamt you into being and knit you together in your mother's womb. I formed your innermost parts with great care and intention, and I deeply love what I have made. When I think of you it brings a smile to my lips and joy to my heart. When I look at you my eyes light up and my heart leaps within me. How I long for you to know and understand the depths and fullness of my love. How I long for you to live your whole life from this deep inner reality. Peter, you are my Beloved . . . am I yours?*

It isn't just any question, it is *the* question: *"Do you truly love me?"* And it isn't just *"Do you truly love me?"* but *"Do you truly love me more than these?"* And what are the *"these"* to which he is referring? Are *"these"* his friends, or his family, or his work, or his business? It could be anything. Which is exactly the point. Because the question Jesus asks Peter isn't just for Peter, it is for us all. Each of us has a different *these*. Jesus wants us to realize that it's only when we live our lives firmly in the center of his love and affection that we are able to be truly free—free of our deep need for love and acceptance and affirmation and significance. Free to *feed his lambs* without *feeding on his lambs*.

Pray

Simply be with Jesus today in prayer. Walk with him on the beach of your soul. Imagine him turning to you and asking you *the* question: *"Do you truly love me more than these?"* Tell him your answer.

Respond

Write a letter to Jesus telling him the answer to his question.

29 – As the Father sent me

Silence

Spend a few minutes in silence allowing your soul and spirit to come to stillness before God. This will prepare your heart both to hear and to receive whatever he may have for you today.

Read

Again Jesus said, "Peace be with you! As the Father has sent me, I am sending you." And with that he breathed on them and said, "Receive the Holy Spirit. If you forgive anyone's sins, their sins are forgiven; if you do not forgive them, they are not forgiven." (John 20:21-23 NIV)

Questions for Reflection

Do you feel *sent* by God? Why or why not?

How does that impact your life?

What does it mean that Jesus is sending you the same way the Father sent him?

How does it help you to know that his Spirit, which he breathed into you, is the one who leads and empowers your life and ministry?

Thoughts

Historically, there are three distinct movements in classic Christianity: foundation, formation, and vocation. Foundation involves what we know to be true about God. It is the information we have learned about God upon which the foundation of our "spiritual house" is built. Ideally, the majority of this foundation comes from God's Word, as it has been read and taught and learned throughout the course of our lifetime. Our spiritual foundation is what everything else rests upon, which means that it is incredibly important.

Formation has to do with a different kind of *knowing*. Our spiritual formation involves what we know about God in the relational sense. It is what we *know* about him from our own experience of him. It is a very intimate kind of *knowing*, similar to the kind of *knowing* mentioned in Genesis 4:1 where it says that Adam *knew* Eve and she conceived a son. This is the kind of *knowing* that God really desires with each of us, a *knowing* more intimate that anything we have ever dreamt of. It involves the very life of God being formed within us by his Spirit.

Vocation is how this life of the Spirit is expressed, or fleshed out, in our lives and in our world. It involves not only how we live, but what our calling and our purpose is as people made in the image of God. Our vocation is not merely our job, but our mission. It is to recognize that our main purpose here on earth is his kingdom and his glory. All three of these movements are obviously vital to the life of faith.

In these verses (John 20:21-23) Jesus is emphasizing the third part of this dance—our vocation. He is giving the disciples—before he departs and returns to the Father—a clear vision of their mission and calling. And he does it with some amazing words: *"As the Father has sent me, I am sending you."* So, from that moment on, they are *sent* people. They are people on a mission. They are the hands and feet (and voices) of Jesus, sent in his name and empowered by his Spirit to love and serve and care for this lost and hurting world. As are we.

As the Father sent me to empty myself and take on the form of a servant, I am now sending you. As the Father sent me to meet people on their turf, to love them in their own world, and to speak about his love in their own language, I am now sending you. As the Father sent me to be the visible expression of the invisible God, I am now sending you. As the Father sent me to seek and save the lost, I am now sending you. As the Father sent me to love the poor and the broken and the marginal, I am now sending you.

That's what true ministry is all about: foundation, formation, and vocation. It is about knowing and loving Jesus with everything in us and loving others as a direct result. It is about being captured by God and then being sent to those in our world. It is when heart and soul and spirit are so full of God that they simply overflow, spilling over and drenching all who are near with the life and fullness of God. That is ministry. Now, let us go and do that!

Pray
Pray for a true sense of being *sent* by God into this day.

Respond
What does it mean, specifically, to be *sent* by God today?

30 – Strong toward

Silence

Spend a few minutes in silence allowing your heart and soul to become still and quiet. This will create good space within you to truly be with Jesus.

Read

When the people heard this, they were cut to the heart and said to Peter and the other apostles, "Brothers, what shall we do?"

Peter replied, "Repent and be baptized, every one of you, in the name of Jesus Christ for the forgiveness of your sins. And you will receive the gift of the Holy Spirit. The promise is for you and your children and for all who are far off—for all whom the Lord our God will call."

With many other words he warned them; and he pleaded with them, "Save yourselves from this corrupt generation." Those who accepted his message were baptized, and about three thousand were added to their number that day.

They devoted themselves to the apostles' teaching and to fellowship, to the breaking of bread and to prayer. Everyone was filled with awe at the many wonders and signs performed by the apostles. All the believers were together and had everything in common. They sold property and possessions to give to anyone who had need. Every day they continued to meet together in the temple courts. They broke bread in their homes and ate together with glad and sincere hearts, praising God and enjoying the favor of all the people. And the Lord added to their number daily those who were being saved. (Acts 2:37-47 NIV)

Questions for Reflection:

What has *cut you to the heart* lately? How or why?

What does the word *repent* mean to you?

What are the things the early church *devoted themselves to?*
Why?

Is each one of those four things present in your life? How?

What will you *devote yourself to* as we come to the end of
this thirty-day journey?

What has been most helpful the past thirty days?

How will you arrange your life in such a way that these things are a part of your regular rhythm?

Thoughts

There is an old saying that goes, *"If you aim at nothing, you will hit it every time."* That statement couldn't be more true, especially when we are talking about the spiritual life. One of the biggest enemies of spiritual growth is a lack of intentionality. Spiritual maturity doesn't take place by accident, it must be something that we thoughtfully and prayerfully aim at and plan toward. If we want to live in an intimate relationship with God, it will not just fall on our heads (as Richard Foster once said). We will have to arrange our lives in certain ways.

The early church knew this. That's why after Peter's sermon, when thousands turned and followed Jesus, they decided to devote themselves to certain things in an effort to move toward a deeper, richer life with him. As a matter of fact, the literal words in the Greek for *devoted themselves to* mean to be *strong toward*. Somehow, somewhere they got together and decided what things they needed to be *strong toward* in order to nurture this new life of faith that they had just begun.

The four things were: the apostles' teaching, the community, the breaking of the bread, and the prayers. These things would be a constant and consistent part of their life together. They would make space regularly for the Word to be spoken to them and take shape within them. They would take special care to make sure they were journeying together in community — having real, authentic, loving, and caring relationships. They would set times and places to take the Lord's Supper together, in order to make sure that the cross of Jesus was a regular focal point of their communal life. And they would gather at appointed times during the day and night (*Seven times a day I will praise you — Psalm 119:164*) to pray. This would be the rhythm their community would operate by to ensure that they were not *aiming at nothing*.

What about you? As we end this thirty-day journey together, what will be next for you? What have you done in the last thirty days that has been life-giving and helpful in your journey with Jesus? How will you integrate those things into your life as you look forward? What are the things you need to be *strong toward* in order to make space for this *life of God within you* to continue to grow and be nurtured?

Pray

Pray that God would give you direction as you consider how he might want you to arrange your life with him. Ask him what things he wants you to be strong toward in this season of your life with him.

Respond

What will you *be strong toward* in the days, weeks, and months ahead? Write down, as specifically as you can, what that will look like.

Conclusion

Well, this is the end of our journey together. I hope it was a rich and meaningful time for you. As a final exercise, spend some time reflecting on the thirty days as a whole:

What has God done in you?

How has he "shown up"?

How are you different now than you were when we began?

How have you grown in the art of *being with Jesus?*

My hope is that, if nothing else, you have gotten a little taste of what it is like to simply be *with* him — to listen to his voice, to look into his eyes, and to sit in his presence. Because I firmly believe that it is through *being with him* that we end up becoming more like him. And, in the end, that's what we are all most deeply longing for. May you know his peace.

63557265R00091